National Test Practice Papers

Maths, English and Science

**Age 10–11
Levels 3–5**

Key Stage 2

Hilary Koll and Steve Mills,
Ray Barker and
Christine Moorcroft,
Graham Peacock

Acknowledgements

The Publishers would like to thank the following for permission to reproduce copyright material:

Silas Hocking: from *Her Benny* (F. Warne & Co. 1879).

Alison Lassieur: from *The Inuit (Native Peoples)* (Bridgestone Books, an imprint of Capstone Press, 2000).

Marian Swinger: 'The First Christmas' from *Read Me 2: A Poem For Every Day Of The Year,* edited by Gaby Morgan (Macmillan Children's Books, 1999), reprinted by permission of the author.

Laura Ingalls Wilder: from *Little House in the Big Woods* (Harper & Row, 1932; Egmont Books, 2009), text copyright 1932, Laura Ingalls Wilder. Copyright renewed 1959 Roger L. MacBride. Published by Egmont UK Ltd London and used with permission.

Every effort has been made to trace all copyright holders, but if any have been inadvertently overlooked the Publishers will be pleased to make the necessary arrangements at the first opportunity.

Although every effort has been made to ensure that website addresses are correct at time of going to press, Hodder Education cannot be held responsible for the content of any website mentioned in this book. It is sometimes possible to find a relocated web page by typing in the address of the home page for a website in the URL window of your browser.

Hachette UK's policy is to use papers that are natural, renewable and recyclable products and made from wood grown in sustainable forests. The logging and manufacturing processes are expected to conform to the environmental regulations of the country of origin.

Orders: please contact Bookpoint Ltd, 130 Milton Park, Abingdon, Oxon OX14 4SB. Telephone: (44) 01235 827720. Fax: (44) 01235 400454. Lines are open 9.00a.m.–5.00p.m., Monday to Saturday, with a 24-hour message answering service. Visit our website at www.hoddereducation.co.uk.

© Hilary Koll and Steve Mills, Ray Barker and Christine Moorcroft, Graham Peacock 2013
First published in 2008 exclusively for WHSmith by
Hodder Education
An Hachette UK Company
338 Euston Road
London NW1 3BH

This second edition first published in 2013 exclusively for WHSmith by Hodder Education.

Impression number   10 9 8 7 6 5 4 3
Year   2018 2017 2016 2015 2014 2013

Cover illustration by Oxford Designers and Illustrators Ltd
Typeset by DC Graphic Design Ltd, Swanley Village, Kent
Printed in Spain

A catalogue record for this title is available from the British Library.

ISBN: 978 1444 189 209

NOTE: The tests, questions and advice in this book are not reproductions of the official test materials sent to schools. The official testing process is supported by guidance and training for teachers in setting and marking tests and interpreting the results. The results achieved in the tests in this book may not be the same as are achieved in the official tests.

Contents

End of Key Stage Assessments

Children who attend state schools in England are assessed at the ages of 7, 11 and 14 as they approach the end of Key Stages 1, 2 and 3 respectively. They are assessed through tasks, tests and by teacher assessments throughout the year. Each child's level is reported to his or her parents/guardians and the collective information about pupils' levels is used to monitor schools.

Key Stage	Year	Age by end of year	National Tests
1 (KS1)	1	6	Phonics Screening Check
	2	7	National Curriculum Statutory tasks and tests
2 (KS2)	3	8	Optional Year 3
	4	9	Optional Year 4
	5	10	Optional Year 5
	6	11	National Curriculum Statutory tasks and tests
3 (KS3)	7	12	Optional Year 7
	8	13	Optional Year 8
	9	14	Optional Year 9

All children in their final year of Key Stage 1 are assessed using the statutory National Curriculum tasks and tests, administered to all eligible children who are working at Level 1 or above in reading, writing and mathematics. Tasks and tests are designed to help inform the final teacher assessment judgement reported for each child at the end of Key Stage 1. These assessments can be carried out at any point during the year up to the end of June.

At the end of **Key Stage 2**, 11-year-olds sit statutory National Curriculum tests during a week in May. In mathematics these include two written papers for children working up to Level 5 and a mental maths test. There is an optional Level 6 test, involving two papers, which exceptionally able children can be submitted for. Children are often assessed in the intervening years using Optional tests in Years 3, 4 and 5, which can help to prepare them for the end of Key Stage tests.

There are two sets of practice papers for each subject in this book. Whilst these WHSmith practice papers might not give exactly the same results as national tests or assessments they can give an indication of the child's attainment and progress and highlight any areas that need more practice.

Levels

National average levels have been set for children's results in the National Tests. The levels are as follows:

LEVEL	AGE 7 (Key Stage 1)	AGE 11 (Key Stage 2)	AGE 14 (Key Stage 3)
8			
7			
6			
5			
4			
3			
2			
2a			
2b			
2c			
1			

☐ BELOW EXPECTED LEVEL

☐ EXPECTED LEVEL

☐ ABOVE EXPECTED LEVEL

☐ EXCEPTIONAL

What can parents do to help?

While it is never a good idea to encourage cramming, you can help your child to succeed by:

- making sure he or she has enough food, sleep and leisure time during the test period
- practising important skills such as writing and reading stories, spelling and mental maths
- telling him or her what to expect in the test, such as important symbols and key words
- helping him or her to be comfortable in test conditions including working within a time limit, reading questions carefully and understanding different ways of answering.

Maths at Key Stage 2

The Key Stage 2 National Tests cover Number, Measures, Shape and Space, and Data Handling. Most children will take two 45-minute written tests and a short, orally delivered mental test. Test A is a written non-calculator paper and Test B is a written paper where children can use a calculator, should they wish. This book contains two sets of practice papers.

Levels

Children taking the Maths Tests A and B and the Mental Maths Test can achieve below Level 3, Level 3, Level 4 or Level 5, with a typical 11-year-old attaining Level 4.

To gain an idea of the level at which your child is working, use the table on pages 26 and 52, which shows you how to convert your child's marks into a National Curriculum Level.

Setting the tests

Written tests

Allow 45 minutes for each test. Do not expect your child to take them one after another. In the National Test week, children will take the mathematics tests over two or three days.

Your child will need a ruler, pencil, eraser, protractor and, if possible, a small mirror or piece of tracing paper, together with a calculator (for Test B).

Encourage your child to work systematically through each test, returning later to questions which cause difficulty.

If your child has difficulty in reading the questions, you can read them aloud, provided the mathematical words are not altered or explained. Where necessary, your child can dictate answers and these can be written down for him or her. For large numbers, however, your child should be clear which digits are intended to be written, e.g. for a number such as three thousand and six, your child should indicate that this is written as three, zero, zero, six.

Mental Maths Tests

The mental test should take approximately 10–15 minutes to give, by reading aloud the questions on pages 20 and 45–46, which you should copy for your own use while your child writes on pages 21 and 47. Your child will only need a pencil and an eraser for the mental test.

Allow only the time suggested for each question. You may read each one twice within this time.

Marking the tests

Next to each question in the written tests is a number indicating how many marks the question or part of the question is worth. Enter your child's mark into the circle above this, using the answer pages (22–25 and 48–51) to help you decide how many points to award.

Find your child's total score from the written tests and mental test, then refer to pages 26 and 52 for information about the level your child might be working at.

1 Fill in the missing numbers.

a $24 \div \boxed{0} = 24 \times 1$

b $16 + 12 = 39 - \boxed{11}$ ✓

c $(3 \times 15) - \boxed{10} = 20 + \boxed{15}$ ✓

2 Write two more numbers into this diagram so that the numbers in each row and column add up to 100.

60 10 30 ✓

10 40 50 ✓

30 50 20

3 a Continue this sequence.

1   3   6   10 $\boxed{15}$ $\boxed{21}$ ✓

b Explain how you worked out the missing numbers.

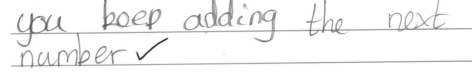

you keep adding the next
number ✓

4   At a netball tournament there are **7** players in each team.

24 teams take part in the tournament.

How many players take part in the tournament?

168 ✓

2

2

5   Lucy is playing darts. She throws three darts and hits
three different numbers. She notices that the **mean**
of the numbers is **7**.

What **different** numbers could Lucy have hit?

10   7   8   ✗ 6,7,8

0

1

TOTAL

2

3

6   A shop sells ice cream.

This table shows the most popular
types of ice cream sold in the shop during one day.

Flavour	Large cone	Small cone
Toffee	21	11
Orange	16	9
Lemon	14	10

1

1

a   How many **small** cones
     were sold during the day?

30 ✓

b   Which flavour had 32 cones
     sold during the day?

 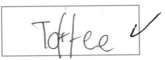
Toffee ✓

2

2

7   One side of a shape has been drawn below. The shape has
     three right angles and **more than four** sides. Using
     a ruler, draw the other sides to complete the shape.

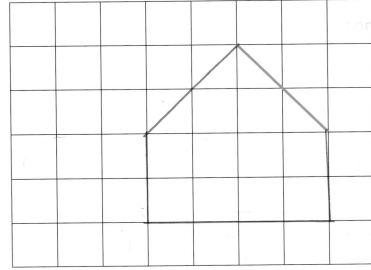

✓

TOTAL

4

4

8 Mr Thomas bought three shirts.

a One shirt cost £10.50. The second shirt cost half as much.

How much did the second shirt cost?

 £ S.25 ✓

 1
1

b Mr Thomas spent exactly £20 on all three shirts.

How much did the third shirt cost?

 £ 4.25 ✓

 1
1

9 Fill in the missing numbers so the numbers along all three sides have the same total.

 0
2

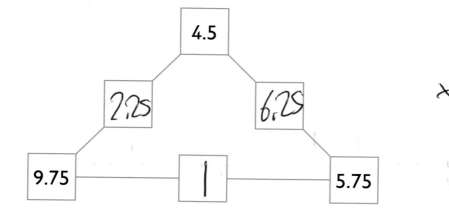

4.5

2.25   6.25

x

9.75   1   5.75

 TOTAL

 2
4

5

10 Playing cards come in different suits.

diamonds   **clubs**   **spades**   **hearts**

Here are five playing cards.

  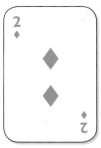 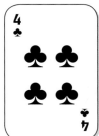 

These five cards are shuffled and spread out face down on a table. **One card** is picked from them.

a What is the probability that it is a **club**?
Give your answer as a fraction.

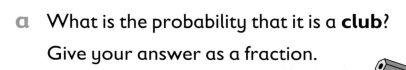 1/4 ✗

b What is the probability that it is a **three**?
Show your answer by drawing a cross on this line.

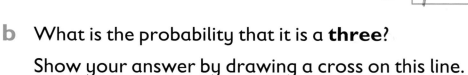

0   1

11 The hundreds digits are missing from two numbers in this number sentence. Write what they could be.

4 5 9 + 3 7 4 = 833 ✓

0
1

1
1

1
1

TOTAL

2

3

12 Look at this multiplication fact.

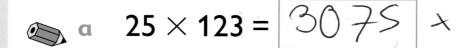

$$26 \times 123 = 3198$$

Use this fact to find the answers to these questions:

a $\quad 25 \times 123 = $ `3075` ✗ 0 / 1

b $\quad 26 \times 124 = $ `3224` ✗ 0 / 1

c $\quad 260 \times 123 = $ `31980` ✗ 0 / 1

d $\quad 2.6 \times 12.3 = $ `3198` ✗ 0 / 1

13 Circle **two** numbers below that are equivalent.

0.4 $\quad \dfrac{3}{4} \quad$ 0.9 $\quad \dfrac{4}{7} \quad \dfrac{7}{10}$ ✗

$\dfrac{2}{5} \quad$ 0.8 $\quad \dfrac{1}{4}$

 0 / 1

14 Calculate **783 − 491** `292`

TOTAL  0 / 6

15 a Using a ruler, and a mirror or tracing paper, **draw and shade** the reflection of the shape below in the mirror line.

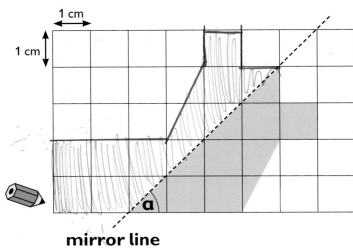

mirror line

2

b What area of the grid is now shaded?

16 cm² ✗

1

c What fraction of the grid is now shaded?

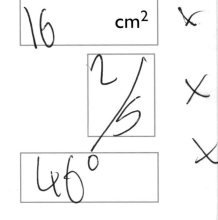 2/5 ✗

1

d How many degrees is **angle a**? You may use an angle measurer (protractor).

46° ✗

1

16 A grocery shop has a delivery of 120 kg of vegetables. 60% of these are potatoes. What is the weight of potatoes?

2

2
70 kg

17 In a gymnastics competition, the gymnasts are awarded points for **difficulty**, **style** and **technical merit**. These points are added together to find a total score.

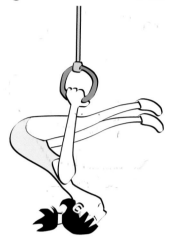

Here are the numbers of points awarded to three children.

Name	Difficulty	Style	Technical merit
Alice	3.8	5.1	4.7
Ajay	4.3	4.9	5.2
Emily	5.4	4.6	4.8

a What is the **total** number of points awarded for **style**?

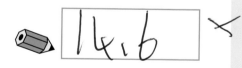

b Which of Ajay's marks is closest to 5 points?

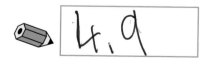

c Whose total score is 14.8?

 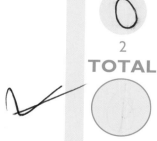

TOTAL

4

9

18 Mrs Wood is buying some fruit.

The fruit comes in bags of different sizes. This table shows the prices of the different bags.

	Bananas	**Apples**
500 g	69p	35p
750 g	99p	50p
1 kg	£1.25	65p

Mrs Wood buys **three bags** of fruit. She buys **one** 500 g bag, **one** 750 g bag and **one** 1 kg bag.

a What is the total **mass** of fruit she buys?

1kg 250g ✓

b She spends a total of **£2.33**.

Which **three** bags of fruit does she buy?

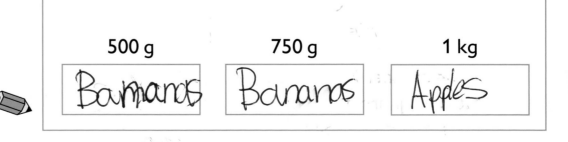

500 g	750 g	1 kg
Bananas	Bananas	Apples

1

2

TOTAL

3

STOP HERE AND MARK THE TEST

1 Write three numbers to make the number sentence correct.

$$\boxed{60} - \boxed{1} - \boxed{1} = 58$$

1

2 An arrow is pointing to each of the number lines below.
Write the numbers indicated by the arrows in the boxes.

a

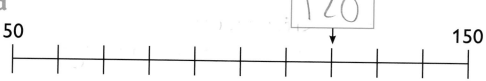

$\boxed{120}$

50 · · · · · · · · · 150

1

b

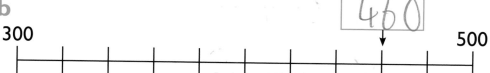

$\boxed{460}$

300 · · · · · · · · · 500

1

c

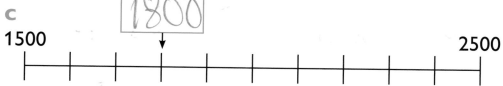

$\boxed{1800}$

1500 · · · · · · · · · 2500

1

3 Here are some number riddles.
Write the number for each riddle in the box.

a

| The number is less than 40. |
| It is a multiple of 6. |
| It is a multiple of 4. |
| It is a multiple of 9. |

$\boxed{36}$

1

1

b

| The number is between 30 and 50. |
| It is a square number. |
| It is an odd number. |

$\boxed{49}$

TOTAL

6

11

4   Write what the **missing numbers** could be to make the number sentences correct.

a $\boxed{26} - \boxed{10} + \boxed{2} = 18$

b $\boxed{9} \div \boxed{-} = 9$

c $6 \times 4 + \boxed{1} = 5 \times \boxed{5}$

1

1

1

5   On Sunday **£4416** was paid by people entering a theme park. They each paid **£12** to get in.

a   How many people went to the theme park on Sunday?

$\boxed{368}$

1

Ice creams cost 75p each.
A **total** of **253** ice creams was bought.

b   How much money was spent on ice creams in total?

$\boxed{189.75}$

2

TOTAL

6

12

6   This diagram shows the **number of kilometres** between some cities in the United Kingdom.

	Aberdeen	Bristol	Glasgow	Manchester	Dover
Aberdeen	—	490	150	332	574
Bristol	490	—	366	167	195
Glasgow	150	366	—	210	467
Manchester	332	167	210	—	265
Dover	574	195	467	265	—

a   Explain why each number appears twice in the table.

Because the teams appear twice

`1`

b   A delivery driver visits three cities on the same journey. She starts at **Glasgow**, drives to **Dover** and then on to **Bristol**. How far does she travel?

662 km

`2`

`1`

7   Use all of these digits to make the four-digit number closest to 6000.

6 9 5 2

5962

TOTAL

`4`

1

8 Here is an arrangement of dots. Join some of these dots with straight lines to draw a **regular hexagon**. Use a ruler.

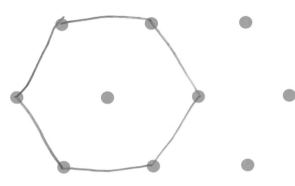

9 Hannah is colouring a flag.

The pattern she is colouring has **rotational symmetry**.

She still has **one square** to colour.

Shade **one** square so that the pattern will have **rotational symmetry**.

1

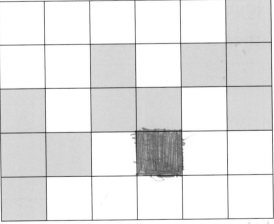

1

TOTAL

10 This number sequence is made by counting on in steps of **equal size**. Fill in the **missing numbers**.

| 6 | 10 | 14 | 18 | 22 |

3

11 David is playing a game using a set of ten **different** number cards showing **1 to 10**. He turns over two cards and adds the numbers to find the **total**.

These are his first four goes:

Card 1	Card 2	Total
6	7	13
3	5	8
4	9	13
7	2	9

a What is the **lowest total** David could possibly get?

 3

1

b Jenny says,
"You are equally likely to get a total of 10 as a total of 3."
Is she correct?
Circle yes or no.

yes	(no)

1

Explain your answer.

 There are more ways to make 10 than three.

1

12 Fill in the missing numbers to make these statements correct.

1

 a 37 674 ÷ | 78 | = 483

1

b 6321 × | 19 | = 120 099

1
TOTAL

4

15

13 Look carefully at the shapes below.

Trapezium

Square

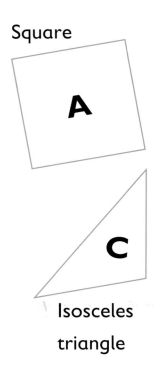

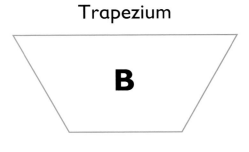

A

B

Regular

octagon

C

D

Isosceles

triangle

Write the letter of shapes **B**, **C** and **D** into the correct section of the table below. A has been done for you.

3

	No pairs of parallel sides	One pair of parallel sides	More than one pair of parallel sides
3 sides	C		
4 sides		B	A
More than 4 sides			D

1

TOTAL

14 Calculate **38%** of **890**.

 210

4

15 Here is a graph.

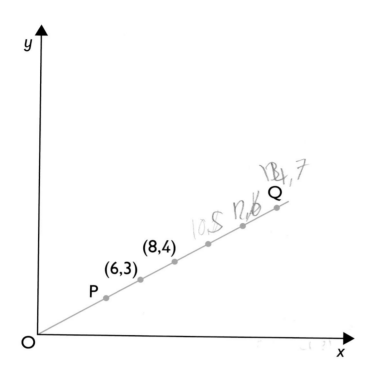

The dots on the line are equally spaced.

a What are the **co-ordinates** of **point Q**?

(13, 7)

2

b Jack says, "The point P has co-ordinates (3,2)".

Explain why he is wrong.

Because its add 2 then

T.

2

TOTAL

4

17

16 Carol is arranging exactly **four** number cards to make different fractions **less than one**. These are the numbers.

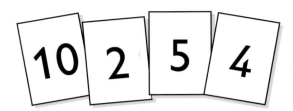

a Using **each** number card only **once**, show where each would go to make this statement correct.

is the same value as

b Find another way to place these cards to make **different** fractions that have the same value.

is the same value as

17 Here is part of a flower bed.

Each flower bed has **342** daffodils. Each row has **19** daffodils in it. How many rows of daffodils are in **8** flower beds?

144

TOTAL

18 Jack and Chloe go to a car boot sale. They buy some books.

Entrance fee 75p and 20p for each book

a Jack pays the **entrance fee** and buys **twelve books**. How much does he spend?

£3.15

1

b Chloe pays the **entrance fee** and buys some books. She spends exactly **£2.55**. How many books does she buy?

2

9

Entrance fee 75p and 20p for each book

c Write a formula to show the total cost (**C**) in pence of visiting the car boot sale if you buy **n** books.

2

TOTAL

C = 20 × n

5

Mental Maths Test 1

Questions

"For this first set of questions you have five seconds to work out each answer and write it down."

1   Write the number three thousand and two in figures.

2   What is twenty-two less than forty?

3   What is half of three point six?

4   Four-tenths of the children in a class are girls. What percentage are girls?

5   How many sides do three octagons have in total?

6   What is half of eighty-four?

"For the next set of questions you have ten seconds to work out each answer and write it down."

7   What is double two hundred and sixty?

8   How many minutes are there in two and a half hours?

9   Add six and eighteen and then divide by four.

10 A snail crawls seventy-two centimetres. How much further does it have to crawl to reach one metre?

11 One-tenth of a number is twenty. What is the number?

12 On the answer sheet is part of a scale. What number is the arrow pointing to?

13 A shop has a sale. All items are twenty-five per cent of their original price. A video costs four pounds in the sale. What was its original price?

14 Sam cycles six miles every day. How far does he cycle in a week?

15 Look at the answer sheet. Draw a ring around the approximate height of a door.

"For the next set of questions you have fifteen seconds to work out each answer and write it down."

16 Look at the answer sheet. Draw a ring around the largest number.

17 Two-fifths of a number is twelve. What is the number?

18 Which year is nineteen years before the year two thousand and eight?

19 Look at the answer sheet. What is the size of angle A?

20 Look at the answer sheet. Draw a ring around three numbers that are multiples of twenty.

5-second questions

1	3002 ✓	4	40% ✓
2	18 ✓	5	24 ✓
3	1.8 ✓	6	42 ✓

6
6

10-second questions

7	520 ✓
8	150 ✓ minutes
9	6 ⌣
10	28 ✓ centimetres
11	200 ✓

12	4.67 ✓

4.6 ↓ 4.7

13	£5 ✗
14	42 ✓ miles

| 15 | 2000 cm   20 m
(200 cm) ✓
20 cm   2 cm |
|---|---|

8
9

15-second questions

| 16 | 0.7   (7.9)   6.6 ✓
7.5   7.74 |
|---|---|
| 17 | 30 ✓ |
| 18 | 1989 ✓ |

19	A = 40° ✓ 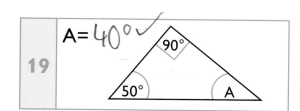

20	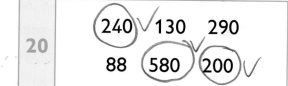

240 ✓ 130 290
88 (580) (200) ✓

5
5

TOTAL
(19)
20

21

Maths Test 1

Question number	Answer	Mark	Parent's notes and additional information
TEST A			
1a	1	1	
1b	11	1	
1c	e.g. 10, 15	1	Two numbers (which add to 25) to make the equation true.
2	10, 40	1	
3a	15, 21	1	
3b	A mark for either: an explanation that the differences between numbers in the sequence go up in ones or a reference to counting on, e.g. "one number missed out, two numbers missed out, etc."	1	Children's answers to questions like these should include <u>numbers</u> to support their explanations. Just writing "I saw a pattern. The numbers go up" is generally not enough to score a mark. These are **triangle** numbers.
4	$24 \times 7 = 168$	2	It does not matter whether this calculation is done mentally or using a written method. One mark for an attempt to multiply 24 by 7.
5	Any three <u>different</u> numbers that have a total of 21, e.g. 6, 7, 8 or 15, 4, 2.	1	The mean (average) of a set of numbers is found by finding the total and dividing this by the number of numbers in the set. In this case there are three numbers so the mean is **21 ÷ 3 = 7**.
6a	30	1	Children are required to interpret the table and then find the total of 11, 9 and 10.
6b	toffee	1	Children should check the total of each row to find the flavour that adds to 32.
7	Any shape with more than four sides and with exactly three right angles. External right angles (those outside the shape) do not count.	2	Examples of shapes: One mark if the shape has more than 4 sides and some right angles.
8a	£5.25 Note that amounts of money should never be written with both the **£** sign and a **p** sign, e.g. £5.25p is incorrect and would not earn a mark.	1	Children must halve £10.50. Children of this age should try to learn doubles of all numbers to 100 and their corresponding halves, e.g. double 25 = 50 and half of 50 = 25. They can then use this knowledge for questions of this kind.
8b	£4.25	1	
9	Any three numbers that make the sides add to same total, e.g. 2.25 at left, 6.25 at right, 1 at base (total 16.5)	2	All three sides should have the same total.
10a	$\frac{1}{5}$	1	There are five cards. The probability of picking the only club is one out of five. Probabilities generally can be written in words or as fractions or decimals, e.g. **one out of five**, $\frac{1}{5}$ or **0.2**.
10b		1	There are five cards. The probability of picking one of the two threes is two out of five = 0.4.
11	Two hundreds digits that add to make 7, e.g. **159 + 674** **259 + 574** **359 + 474** **459 + 374** **559 + 274** or **659 + 174**	1	If your child has written two hundreds digits that add to make 8, encourage him or her to add the two numbers together, e.g. 459 + 474 Point out that the answer comes to 933.
12a	3075	1	Your child should notice that 25 × 123 is 123 less than 26 × 123. Ideally he or she should subtract 123 from 3198 to get 3075. A mark can be awarded if the answer was found using a different method.
12b	3224	1	Again, your child should notice that 26 × 124 is 26 more than 26 × 123. If he or she finds this difficult, discuss it in a context, e.g. 124 things costing £26, cost £26 more than 123 things costing £26.

Question number	Answer	Mark	Parent's notes and additional information
12c	31 980	1	This answer is ten times larger than the given multiplication fact.
12d	31.98	1	Encourage your child to work out an approximate answer to decide where the decimal point should go, e.g. 2.6 × 12.3 is approximately **3 × 12** = 36, so the answer is not 319.8 or 3.198, but 31.98.
13	0.4 and $\frac{2}{5}$ are equivalent	1	Equivalent means that they have the same value, e.g. 0.4 of a metre is the same length as $\frac{2}{5}$ of a metre.
14	292	1	
15a		2	Award one mark if five or six out of the seven corners of the shape are reflected correctly.
15b	16 cm^2	1	The area of a shape is the number of whole squares inside the shape. In this case it is centimetre squares or cm^2 that are counted. If your child gave the answer 22, he or she counted half squares as whole squares.
15c	$\frac{16}{40}$ or $\frac{8}{20}$ or $\frac{4}{10}$ or $\frac{2}{5}$	1	There should be 16 out of 40 squares shaded.
15d	45° Accept answers that are 1 degree either side of 45°, i.e. 44° or 46°.	1	A protractor is not essential for this question. Show your child that the angle is half a right angle and that the exact answer is 90 ÷ 2 = 45°.
16	72 kg	2	Award one mark for workings that show 10% of 120 = 12. To find 60% of 120, first find 10% of 120. 120 ÷ 10 = 12. Then multiply 12 by 6 to find 60%. 12 × 6 = 72.
17a	14.6	1	5.1 + 4.9 + 4.6
17b	4.9 (for Style)	1	Children may incorrectly answer 5.2. Show that 5.2 is two-tenths away from 5 whereas 4.9 is one-tenth away from 5.
17c	Emily	2	3.8 + 5.1 + 4.7 = 13.6 4.3 + 4.9 + 5.2 = 14.4 5.4 + 4.6 + 4.8 = 14.8 Award one mark for workings that show some correct addition of scores.
18a	2250 g or 2.25 kg	1	500 g + 750 g + 1 kg (1000 g)
18b	500 g bananas (69p), 750 g bananas (99p), 1 kg apples (65p).	2	This question involves interpreting information and dealing with two criteria: the price (£2.33) and the different masses of the bags. Award one mark for attempts to add sets of three numbers, including prices and masses.
TEST B			
1	Any three numbers that make the sentence correct: 60 − 1 − 1, 70 − 10 − 2, etc.	1	
2a	120	1	Show your child that the 100 is split into 10 sections, so each must be worth 10.
2b	460	1	Show your child that the 200 is split into 10 sections, so each must be worth 20.
2c	1800	1	Show your child that the 1000 is split into 10 sections, so each must be worth 100.
3a	36	1	A multiple is a number that can be divided exactly without a remainder, e.g. multiples of 6 include 6, 12, 18, 180, 486, etc.
3b	49	1	A square number is a number that is made from multiplying another number by itself, e.g. 4 = 2 × 2, 9 = 3 × 3, 25 = 5 × 5. Children should learn the square numbers to 100, i.e. 1, 4, 9, 16, 25, 36, 49, 64, 81, 100.
4a	Any three numbers that make the sentence equal 18, e.g. 30 − 15 + 3, 50 − 40 + 8.	1	

Question number	Answer	Mark	Parent's notes and additional information
4b	Any numbers that divide to make 9, e.g. 9 ÷ 1, 18 ÷ 2, 27 ÷ 3.	1	
4c	Any numbers that make the statement correct, e.g. $6 \times 4 + \mathbf{1} = 5 \times \mathbf{5}$ $6 \times 4 + \mathbf{6} = 5 \times \mathbf{6}$ $6 \times 4 + \mathbf{11} = 5 \times \mathbf{7}$.	1	Children often find this type of question difficult because they see the equals sign as an "answer giver" rather than meaning "is/has the same answer as". Here $6 \times 4 + \square$ "has the same answer as" $5 \times \square$. Also, 6×4 must be multiplied before adding the missing number.
5a	368	1	$4416 \div 12$
5b	£189.75	2	Here children must be aware of their actions if they multiply by 0.75 or 75. If they multiply by 0.75 their answer will be in pounds but if they multiply by 75 their answer will be in pence so they will need to divide by 100.
6a	Any explanation showing that your child appreciates that the distance between two towns, e.g. Bristol to Dover, will be the same distance in reverse, e.g. Dover to Bristol.	1	
6b	662 km	2	A common mistake is to select the incorrect second distance. If your child answered 833 km, it is because he or she used the distances between Glasgow and Dover (467) and then between <u>Glasgow</u> and Bristol (366), rather than Glasgow and Dover (467) and on from <u>Dover</u> to Bristol (195). Award one mark if the working shows 467 + 195, but with an incorrect answer.
7	5962	1	
8	A regular hexagon has six equal sides and six equal angles.	1	
9		1	Shapes or patterns that have rotational symmetry can look the same in more than one orientation when turned. Letters like S, H, X, O have rotational symmetry, but A, E, T, W do not. They cannot be turned to look the same in any other orientation.
10	10, 14, 22	1	To answer this question, your child should find the difference between 18 and 6 = 12. If the difference between boxes that are three apart is 12 then the difference between each box is 12 ÷ 3 = 4.
11a	3	1	David can pick a 1 and a 2 card, with a total of 3.
11b	no There must be an explanation with reference to the fact that there are more ways to make 10 than there are to make 3, e.g. 3 can only be scored with a 1 and a 2 card, whereas 10 can be scored with a 1 and 9, 2 and 8, 3 and 7 or 6 and 4.	1	Children's answers to questions like these should include <u>numbers</u>, where possible. It is not enough to say that "it is more likely to score 10 than 3".
12a	78	1	Children often attempt questions of this type using trial and error, e.g. trying to divide 37 674 by different numbers to get 483. This involves a great deal of time. Instead, encourage your child to see that division questions can be rearranged, e.g. 10 ÷ 5 = 2 and 10 ÷ 2 = 5. Here children should divide 37 674 by 483 to get 78.
12b	19	1	Again, children attempt questions of this type using trial and error, e.g. trying to multiply 6321 by different numbers to get 120 099. Instead, encourage your child to see that multiplication questions can be rearranged, e.g. 2 × 5 = 10 can be rearranged to make 10 ÷ 2 = 5. Here children should divide 120 099 by 6321 to get 19.

Question number	Answer	Mark	Parent's notes and additional information
13	C B A D (grid)	3	Parallel lines are lines that, if extended in either direction, would never meet. Parallel lines are the same distance apart. A regular shape has equal sides and equal angles. Award one mark for each of the letters B, C and D correctly positioned.
14	338.2	1	38% of 890 can be worked out in the following ways: $38 \div 100 \times 890$ $38 \times 890 \div 100$ 0.38×890
15a	(14 , 7)	2	Award 1 mark for each correct co-ordinate.
15b	An explanation suggesting that all points along the line have a first (x) co-ordinate twice the second (y) co-ordinate so (3, 2) cannot lie along the line.	2	
16a	$\frac{4}{10}$ and $\frac{2}{5}$ or $\frac{2}{4}$ and $\frac{5}{10}$	1	The fractions can be in any order, e.g. $\frac{2}{5}$ and $\frac{4}{10}$ or $\frac{4}{10}$ and $\frac{2}{5}$.
16b	$\frac{4}{10}$ and $\frac{2}{5}$ or $\frac{2}{4}$ and $\frac{5}{10}$	1	Do <u>not</u> award a mark if the answer has the same fractions as question 16a, even if given in a different order.
17	144	2	Award one mark for a method that shows $342 \div 19 \times 8$, but with an incorrect answer.
18a	£3.15 Do <u>not</u> award a mark for the answer £3.15p or £315.	1	Money answers must be written correctly for questions of this type. Calculator questions like these are often selected to see whether children can interpret the display in the context of money. Amounts of money should never be written with both the £ sign and a p sign.
18b	9	2	Children may incorrectly answer 12.75 or 13. Remind them that the entrance fee (75p) should be subtracted first. Award one mark for attempts to subtract 75 from 255 and divide this by 20.
18c	Any of the following answers: $C = 75 + (20 \times n)$ $C = 75 + (n \times 20)$ $C = 75 + 20n$ $C = 20n + 75$ $C = 20 \times n + 75$ etc. Award one mark for $C = 20n$ or $C = 20 \times n$	2	Children find using letters in place of numbers quite difficult. Show them the following: For 1 book $C \text{ (cost)} = 75 + (1 \times 20)$ For 2 books $C \text{ (cost)} = 75 + (2 \times 20)$ For 3 books $C \text{ (cost)} = 75 + (3 \times 20)$, etc. So for n books $C \text{ (cost)} = 75 + (n \times 20)$.

Answers

Mental Maths Test 1

1. 3002	6. 42	11. 200	16. 7.9
2. 18	7. 520	12. 4.67	17. 30
3. 1.8	8. 150 minutes	13. £16	18. 1989
4. 40%	9. 6	14. 42 miles	19. 40°
5. 24	10. 28 cm	15. 200 cm	20. 240, 580, 200

One mark per correct answer.

National Curriculum Levels

Maths Test 1

Write your child's scores in the Maths Tests below.

Mark scored in Test 1A   [   ]   out of 40

Mark scored in Test 1B   [   ]   out of 40

Mark scored in Mental Maths Test 1   [   ]   out of 20

Total score   [   ]   out of 100

The National Tests are levelled according to the child's total score.

Mark	0–24	25–51	52–79	80–100
Level	1/2	3	4	5

For each test this can be broadly broken down as follows:

TEST 1A	Mark	0–10	11–20	21–31	32–40
	Level	1/2	3	4	5

TEST 1B	Mark	0–10	11–20	21–31	32–40
	Level	1/2	3	4	5

MENTAL TEST 1	Mark	0–4	5–10	11–15	16–20
	Level	1/2	3	4	5

1 Fill in the missing numbers.

 a $36 \div \boxed{9} = 4$

 b $48 - 16 = 21 + \boxed{12}$

 c $(3 \times 7) - \boxed{15} = 12 + \boxed{8}$

1

1

1

2 Arrange these numbers in **order of size**, starting with the smallest.

| 517 | 486 | 654 | 571 | 682 |

 $\boxed{486}$ $\boxed{517}$ $\boxed{571}$ $\boxed{654}$ $\boxed{682}$

smallest

1

3 Arrange these four number cards to make a **subtraction** question with an **answer** of **25**.

| 4 | 3 | 9 | 5 |

1

 $\boxed{} - \boxed{} = 25$

TOTAL

5

27

4 Alice buys **three** bags of crisps.

She pays with a **£2 coin** and gets **20p change**.

What is the cost of one bag of crisps?

1.8~~0~~

3⟌1.80 → 0.60

60p

2

5

Boat hire	
Up to 1 hour	£2.50
1 to 2 hours	£3.50
2 to 3 hours	£5.00
3 to 5 hours	£6.00

Matt and Nita hired a boat at 10:30 and returned it at 12:20.

a How much did they pay?

b Katie and Joe hired a boat at **11:20** and paid **£3.50**.

Between which two times might they have returned it?

Between [   ] and [   ]

1

2

TOTAL

5

28

6 This is a spinner on a TV game show.

The contestants spin the pointer to see what prize they will win. The spinner is a regular octagon.

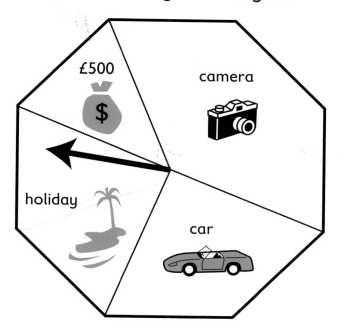

a Draw lines to show how likely these statements are.

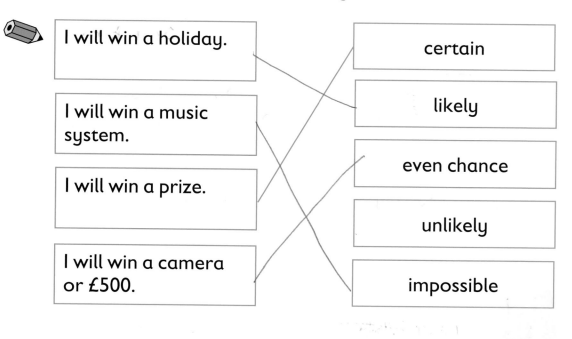

I will win a holiday.	certain
I will win a music system.	likely
I will win a prize.	even chance
	unlikely
I will win a camera or £500.	impossible

3

1

TOTAL

b What is the probability of winning a camera?

Give your answer as a fraction.

4

29

7 **a** What is the order of rotational symmetry of these shapes?

 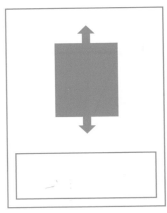 

2

b Sketch a shape with rotational symmetry of **order 4**.

Your shape must NOT be a square.

1

8 The cost of 48 eggs is **£7.20**.

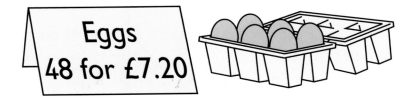

How much does **one egg** cost?

2

TOTAL

5

9 Calculate **763 − 439**.

⁶¹
7̸6̸3 −
439
434

434

1

10 Here is a table of temperatures taken on January 1st in Whitton.

Time	Temperature in Whitton
04:00	−10°C
06:00	−7°C
08:00	−5°C
10:00	−1°C
12:00	4°C
14:00	11°C
16:00	12°C

a How many degrees warmer was it at 14:00 than at 08:00?

16 °C

1

b What is the difference between the highest and lowest temperatures?

22 °C

1

1

c Which two temperatures in the table have a difference of 6°C?

°C | °C

TOTAL

4

11 a On the grid draw a **rectangle** with the **same area** as the shaded triangle.

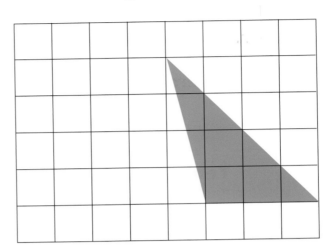

2

b What **fraction** of the grid is now covered by the **triangle and the rectangle**? Give your answer as a fraction in its simplest form.

2

12 Which person is correctly describing this statement?

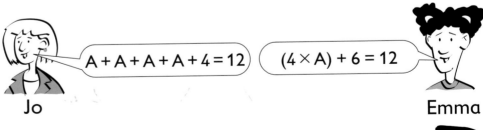

6 less than four lots of A equals 12.

$A + A + A + A + 4 = 12$ $(4 \times A) + 6 = 12$

Jo

Emma

1

$(4 \times A) - 6 = 12$ $A \times A \times A \times A - 6 = 12$

Ali

Rob

13 **Two** numbers in the grid below have a **total of 2**.
Circle both numbers.

0.57	1.42	1.2
0.86	0.71	1.32
1.61	0.4	1.29

1

14 Here is a grid made of squares.

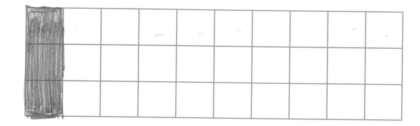

a Shade 10% of this grid.

b **How many more squares** would need to be
shaded to make **two-thirds** of the grid shaded?

17

1

1

15 Mark with arrows the points **0.65** and **−1.3** on the line.

2

TOTAL

5

16 The minute hand on this clock is pointing to the number 10.

a How many **degrees** will it turn clockwise to point to the number 1?

b Starting at the number 10, which **number** will the minute hand point to after a clockwise turn of **120°**?

c Starting at the number 10, how many **degrees** will the minute hand turn clockwise to point to the number **9**?

1

1

1

17 Circle THREE numbers that are **multiples of 6**.

1

TOTAL

 102   64   128   96   56   78

4

34

18 This table shows how many times five children went on the rides at the theme park.

Child's name	Name of ride			
	Swinger	Laser	Cruiser	Saturn
Paul	2	3	1	0
Sunil	0	0	5	1
Ben	1	2	0	4
Sophie	0	1	2	2
Laura	3	3	0	0

a Which of these two rides was more popular – **Swinger** or **Saturn**?  Saturn

1

This chart shows the number of times that **four** of the children went on the different rides. **One child's** information has been missed off the chart.

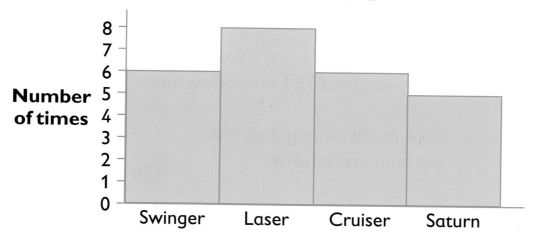

b Which child's information has been missed off this chart?

1

c Explain how you worked this out.

_____

_____

_____

1

TOTAL

3

1 Fill in the **missing numbers** to make the number sentences correct.

 a ☐ − 54 = 37

 b 592 ÷ ☐ = 16

2 Use four **different** numbers to make **both** these number sentences correct.

 ☐ × ☐ = 156

 ☐ × ☐ = 156

3 Lisa works **38** hours every week in an office. She is paid **£323** for each **week**.

a How much money does she get paid every **hour**?

 £ ☐

b Lisa is saving to buy a computer that costs **£1200**. What is the **fewest** number of **weeks** she will have to work to be paid **£1200**?

TOTAL

7

36

4   Here is a glass table with some shapes on it.

Draw how the shapes would look from underneath the table.

2

5   Jack places five number cards on the table.

He closes his eyes and picks **one** card.

a   What is the **probability** that he chooses number **7**? Write your answer as a fraction.

1

b   What is the **probability** that he chooses an even number? Write your answer as a fraction.

1

6   Measure **accurately** the **longest** side of this pentagon in **millimetres**.

 mm

2

TOTAL

6

7 Mr Simpson is cooking some pies in his oven.

This chart shows the temperature inside the oven at different times in the morning.

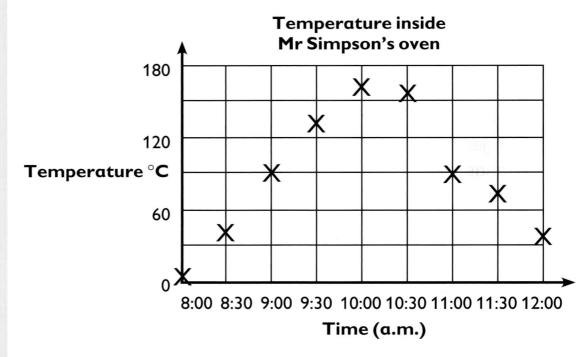

a At what time was the oven at its hottest?

b What was the approximate temperature at 11.30 a.m.?

 °C

c For how long was the oven temperature at or above 90 °C?

Give your answer in minutes.

1

1

1

TOTAL

3

8   Draw a cross on TWO numbers with a **difference of 50**.

(44) (96) (83)

(23) (84) (56)

(74) (46) (63)

1

9   This list shows the cost of fruit at the supermarket.

Fruit	Cost per bag
Apples	£0.89
Pears	£1.20
Oranges	£1.15
Bananas	£0.64
Plums	£1.26

Bob bought **one bag of oranges** and **one bag of apples**. He then bought **one more bag of fruit**.

He spent **£3.30** in total.

Which other bag of fruit did he buy?

2

1

1

10 a   Calculate $\frac{4}{5}$ of 375.

b   Calculate **27%** of £186.    £

TOTAL

5

39

11 Greg wants to hang a painting on the wall between two shelves. One shelf is **64 cm** from the floor.

The other shelf is **180 cm** from the floor.

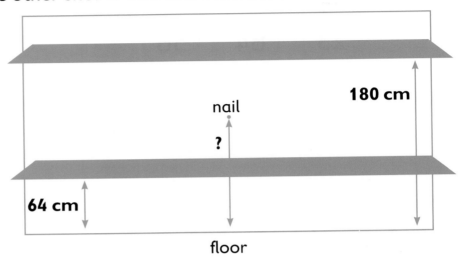

Greg puts the nail **exactly half-way** between the two shelves.

How many **centimetres** from the floor does he put the nail?

cm

2

12 a Circle **two** numbers with a **difference** of 8.

−5   −4   −3   −2   −1   0   1   2   3   4   5

1

b Write two numbers with a sum of −7.

1

TOTAL

4

13 Look at the shapes on the grid.

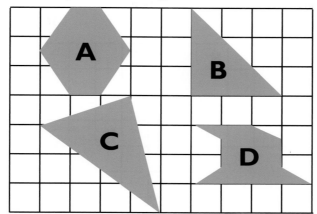

Write one of the letters into each sentence to make it correct.

 a Shape ☐ is a scalene triangle.

1

 b Shape ☐ is an octagon.

1

c Shape ☐ has three pairs of parallel sides.

1

14 There are **9 sweets** in a bag of Whizzos. In every bag **7** are **black** and **2** are **red**.

Megan and Joe buy some bags of Whizzos and tip the sweets onto a table.

There are **28 black sweets** on the table. How many **red sweets** are there?

2

TOTAL

5

15 a A picture of a boat has been reflected and rotated on this grid.

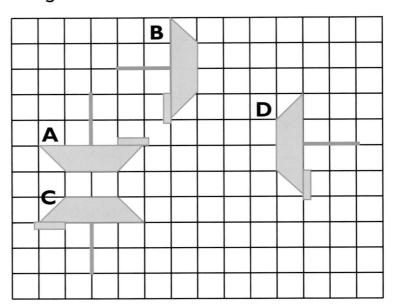

Write the letter of the boat that is a **reflection** of boat **A**.

b Boat E on the grid below is **rotated through two right angles** about the **point P**.

Draw the outline of the rotated shape on the grid below.

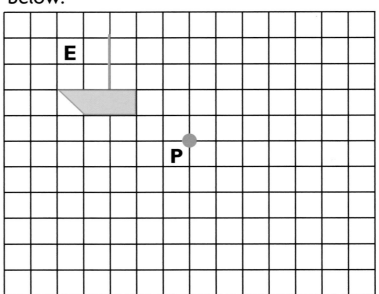

1

2

TOTAL

3

42

16 Jack has a set of cards numbered from **1 to 12**. He turns them face down and picks **four** cards.

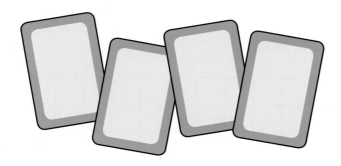

Exactly three of the four numbers are **multiples of 3**.

Exactly three of the four numbers are **odd numbers**.

The total of the four cards is **less than 20**.

What could the four cards be?

3

17 Find the value of the missing number in this equation.

 $\boxed{} \div 3 + 8 = 14$

1

TOTAL

4

18 It has been raining and some puddles have formed. The sun comes out and the puddles begin to dry up.

This graph shows the amount of water in two puddles during several hours.

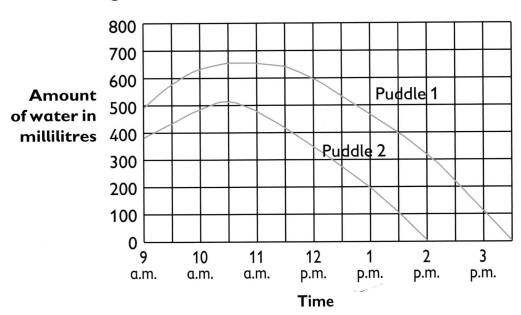

a What time do you think it stopped raining?

1

b At approximately what time was the water in Puddle 1 **four times** as much as in Puddle 2?

1

c Chandu is looking at the graph. She says:

"*Puddle 1 lost 500 ml of water in three hours.*"

Is she correct?

Circle the answer.

 | yes | no |

1

TOTAL

Explain in words why you think this.

_____

_____

3

"For this first set of questions you have five seconds to work out each answer and write it down."

1 What is double thirty-six?

2 What is three times eight then subtract one?

3 Write the number four thousand and four in figures.

4 One blue cube and four white cubes are in a bag. The probability of picking a blue cube is one-fifth. What is the probability of picking a white cube?

5 Multiply seven by nine.

6 How many 10p coins have the same value as three pounds?

"For the next set of questions you have ten seconds to work out each answer and write it down."

7 I start with a five pound note. I spend one pound forty pence. How much have I now?

8 What is the difference between forty-two and seventeen?

9 One-third of a number is eight. What is the number?

10 What is two thousand six hundred grams to the nearest kilogram?

11 Look at the answer sheet. In the equation, what is the value of *x*?

12 James cycles eight miles a week. In how many weeks will he have cycled forty-eight miles?

13 Look at the answer sheet. What is the next number in the sequence?

14 A TV programme started at quarter to six. It finished at twenty past seven. How many minutes did the programme last?

15 Look at the answer sheet. Draw a ring around two fractions equivalent to five-tenths.

"For the next set of questions you have fifteen seconds to work out each answer and write it down."

16 Look at the answer sheet. Here are some ice skating scores. Draw a ring around the name of the person who scored exactly half the score of Sam.

17 One-sixth of a number is twenty. What is the number?

18 Look at the answer sheet. Draw a ring around the largest number.

19 I went to the shop with ten pounds. I spent eighty pence and then one pound and fifteen pence. How much did I have left?

20 Look at the answer sheet. Draw a ring around three numbers that are prime numbers.

5-second questions

1	

4	

2	

5	

3	

6	

6

10-second questions

7	£

12	weeks

8	

13	2 7 12 17 ?

9	

14	minutes

10	kg

11	$x =$	$40 + x = 75$

15	$\dfrac{10}{5}$ $\dfrac{50}{100}$ $\dfrac{1}{2}$ $\dfrac{2}{5}$

9

15-second questions

16	Sam 5.4 points Del 2.2 points Urvi 2.7 points Clive 3.2 points

19	£

17	

20	6 17 12 31 63 53 51 100

18	1.3 4.52 4.6 3.99 3.717

5

TOTAL

20

Answers

Maths Test 2

Question number	Answer	Mark	Parent's notes and additional information
TEST A			
1a	9	1	
1b	11	1	
1c	e.g. 1, 8	1	Two numbers (which add to 9) to make equation true.
2	486, 517, 571, 654, 682	1	
3	59 − 34	1	
4	60p	2	Award one mark for workings that show £2 − 20p = £1.80, and the other mark for 180p ÷ 3 = 60p.
5a	£3.50	1	
5b	Between 12:20 and 13:20	2	Award one mark for each correct time. Accept answers to the nearest minute, e.g. 12:20 or 12:21 and 13:19 or 13:20.
6a		3	Award one mark for each correct line. Children may often answer "likely" for the first situation. Show them that there are more chances of <u>not</u> winning a holiday than of winning a holiday.
6b	$\frac{3}{8}$	1	The spinner can be split into eight equal sections. The camera takes up three of the eight.
7a	1, 2, 5	2	Award one mark if two out of the three answers are correct.
7b	Any shape that can be rotated to fit into its outline in exactly four different ways. The shape must not be a square.	1	Examples include:
8	15p	2	Award one mark if workings show an attempt to divide 720 by 48. Children should realise that 720 ÷ 48 will give an answer in pence.
9	324	1	Children can answer this question using any method. Encourage your child to make a mental approximation, e.g. 750 − 450 = 300. This can help to avoid unnecessary errors.
10a	16 °C	1	Encourage your child to draw or imagine a number line from −5 to 11 and to count from −5 to zero (= 5) and from zero to 11 (= 11) and to find the total.
10b	22 °C	1	Again, encourage your child to draw or imagine a number line, this time from −10 to 12 and to count from −10 to zero (= 10) and from zero to 12 (= 12) and to find the total.
10c	−1 °C, −7 °C	1	

48

Question number	Answer	Mark	Parent's notes and additional information
11a	A rectangle with an area of 6 squares should be drawn. These can be made from part squares provided the total number of squares shaded is 6.	2	To find the area of this triangle, it is best for children to know that its area is half the vertical height of the triangle multiplied by the distance along the bottom of it, e.g. area = $\frac{1}{2}$ (base × vertical height) = $\frac{1}{2}$ (3 × 4) = $\frac{1}{2}$ (12) = 6 Award one mark for a shape other than a rectangle with an area of 6 squares.
11b	$\frac{1}{4}$	2	The triangle has an area of 6 squares and the rectangle should have an area of 6 squares = total area of 12 squares. There are 48 squares in the grid. Award one mark for equivalent fractions such as $\frac{12}{48}$ or $\frac{6}{24}$ or $\frac{3}{12}$
12	Ali	1	
13	0.71 and 1.29	1	
14a	Three squares should be shaded.	1	This question requires children to know that 10% of 30 can be found by dividing 30 by 10.
14b	17	1	This question requires children to know that two-thirds of 30 can be found by finding one-third and multiplying by 2, e.g. 30 ÷ 3 = 10, 10 × 2 = 20. Award a mark if the total number of squares shaded (for part a) and the number given (for part b) have a total of 20.
15		2	
16a	90°	1	
16b	2	1	
16c	330°	1	To turn to reach 10 is four right angles, i.e. 4 × 90 = 360°. This turn is 30° less.
17	102, 96, 78	1	
18a	Saturn	1	
18b	Sophie's	1	On the graph, there is 0 missing from the Swinger column, 1 missing from the Laser column, 2 missing from the Cruiser column and 2 missing from the Saturn column. These are the numbers of times Sophie went on the rides.
18c	Any explanation that refers to reading the graph and looking at the table and counting – even if the answer to 18b is wrong.	1	
TEST B			
1a	91	1	
1b	37	1	Children often attempt questions of this type using trial and error, e.g. trying to divide 592 by different numbers to get 16. This involves a great deal of time. Instead, encourage your child to see that division questions can be rearranged, e.g. 10 ÷ 5 = 2 and 10 ÷ 2 = 5. Here children should divide 592 by 16 to get 37.
2	Solutions such as 78 × 2 or 2 × 78 26 × 6 or 6 × 26 and other answers that multiply to make 156, e.g. 13 × 12	2	Award one mark for each correct solution.

Maths Test 2 – Answers

Question number	Answer	Mark	Parent's notes and additional information
3a	£8.50 Do <u>not</u> award a mark for the answer £8.5 or £8.50p.	1	Money answers must be written correctly for questions of this type. Calculator questions like these are often selected to see whether children can interpret the display in the context of money. Amounts of money should never be written with both the **£** sign and a **p** sign.
3b	4 weeks	2	Children need to divide £1200 by £323 to find the fewest number of weeks. This, however, does not give a whole number of weeks and children must round this number up to the next nearest whole number, i.e. 4. Award one mark for each answer 3.7 or 3.7151 etc.
4		2	Children can use tracing paper or a mirror for questions such as these. Award one mark if one shape is incorrect.
5a	$\frac{1}{5}$	1	Your child should notice that there are five cards and that one of the cards shows a 7. Thus the probability is one out of five. Probabilities generally can be written in words or as fractions or decimals, e.g. **one out of five, $\frac{1}{5}$ or 0.2**.
5b	$\frac{3}{5}$	1	Children should notice that there are five cards and that three of the cards are even. Thus the probability is three out of five.
6	47 mm	2	Award one mark for 46 mm or 48 mm.
7a	10:00 a.m.	1	
7b	75 °C	1	Show your child that each 60 on the vertical axis is split into two sections, so each must be worth 30. Award a mark for any answer within the 73 °C–77 °C range.
7c	120 minutes	1	If your child has answered 2 hours, show him or her that the question asks for the answer in minutes.
8	96, 46	1	
9	Plums	2	Award one mark for £2.04 and an attempt to subtract this from £3.30.
10a	300	1	To find $\frac{4}{5}$ of 375 on a calculator, divide 4 by 5 and multiply by 375, or multiply 375 by 4 and divide by 5.
10b	£50.22	1	27% of 186 can be worked out in the following ways: 27 ÷ 100 186 or 27 × 186 ÷ 100 or 0.27 × 186
11	122 cm	2	Award one mark for an attempt to add the numbers and halve.
12a	−5 and 3, −4 and 4, or −3 and 5	1	
12b	−5 and −2 or −4 and −3	1	
13a	C	1	A scalene triangle is a triangle with no equal sides.
13b	D	1	An octagon has 8 straight sides.
13c	A	1	
14	8	2	This is a ratio question. Each bag has 7 black sweets. If there are 28 black sweets altogether, there must be 4 bags. If there are 4 bags, each with 2 red sweets, there must be 8 red sweets. Award one mark for workings containing information that there are 4 bags of sweets.
15a	B	1	Children can find it difficult to visualise reflections in a diagonal mirror line.

Question number	Answer	Mark	Parent's notes and additional information
15b	Award 1 mark for correct orientation but in wrong place.	2	Tracing paper can be used for questions of this type.
16	1, 3, 6, 9	3	Award two marks for three correct numbers, one mark for two correct numbers.
17	18	1	
18a	10:30 a.m.	1	
18b	1:30 p.m.	1	Puddle 1 was 400 ml and puddle 2 was 100 ml.
18c	Yes. An explanation with reference to between 12 p.m. and 3 p.m., going from 600 ml to 100 ml.	1	

Answers
Mental Maths Test 2

1. 72
2. 23
3. 4004
4. $\frac{4}{5}$ or four-fifths
5. 63
6. 30
7. £3.60
8. 25
9. 24
10. 3 kg
11. 35
12. 6 weeks
13. 22
14. 95 minutes
15. $\frac{50}{100}$, $\frac{1}{2}$
16. Urvi, 2.7 points
17. 120
18. 4.6
19. £8.05
20. 17, 31, 53

One mark per correct answer

Write your child's scores in the Maths Tests below.

Mark scored in Test 2A [ ] out of 40

Mark scored in Test 2B [ ] out of 40

Mark scored in Mental Maths Test 2 [ ] out of 20

Total score [ ] out of 100

The National Tests are levelled according to the child's total score.

Mark	24 or below	25–51	52–79	80–100
Level	1/2	3	4	5

For each test this can be broadly broken down as follows:

TEST 2A	Mark	0–10	11–20	21–31	32–40
	Level	1/2	3	4	5

TEST 2B	Mark	0–10	11–20	21–31	32–40
	Level	1/2	3	4	5

MENTAL TEST 2	Mark	0–4	5–10	11–15	16–20
	Level	1/2	3	4	5

The Reading Test at Key Stage 2 comprises a variety of texts – non-fiction, fiction and poetry – to test reading strategies across a range of genres. There will normally be a common theme.

The questions require four different kinds of answers:

- Short words or phrases (one mark for each correct response).
- Longer answers (one or two sentences) which require more understanding of the text (two or more marks).
- Detailed explanations of opinion (up to three marks).
- Multiple choice (one mark).

Although some questions will have a "right answer", all children will express their responses in a different way. Marking guidelines are given on pages 77–78 and an indication of National Curriculum Levels on page 80.

Setting the test

Allow 15 minutes for reading the passages (when no writing is allowed) and 45 minutes for answering the questions.

1. Encourage your child to read the introduction on the next page and each passage carefully.
2. Point out the different types of questions: those which give a choice of answers to tick and those which need a written answer. Written answers need not be complete sentences. Some written answers are worth three or more marks if detail or examples are required.
3. Do not help your child to read the text, although you may help with the spelling of the answers.
4. Point out that your child may rub out or alter any mistakes.
5. Tell your child:
   - to find the answers in the text, rather than guessing;
   - to tick only one box in multiple choice questions;
   - to try to answer every question;
   - to leave any questions he or she cannot answer and go back to them at the end;
   - to re-read the text to find the answers.

Different views of Christmas

Contents

Non-fiction: **Christmas Celebrations**

Fiction: **Christmas Eve**

Poetry: **The First Christmas**

Christmas means different things to different people.

In these extracts, we look at different people's experiences and views of Christmas:

- from an information text about what Christmas means to Christians (a website to which people from different countries sent information);

- from a novel set about 130 years ago;

- from a twentieth-century poem.

You have **15 minutes** to read through these three passages, and **45 minutes** to answer the questions.

Christmas Celebrations

People around the world celebrate Christmas in different ways, both religious and non-religious. Many celebrations are based on legends and traditions which pre-date Christianity, and important dates in the Christian calendar (such as Epiphany, on 6 January) are sometimes linked with the dates of pagan festivals. Many celebrations include the traditional foods of a country and many are influenced by the climate of the country.

Mexico

As Christmas approaches, elaborately decorated market stalls are set up in town centres to sell crafts, foods such as cheese, bananas, nuts and cookies, and flowers such as orchids and poinsettias.

There is a legend about the poinsettia. A little boy gathered some green branches from along the roadside while he was walking to church to look at the Nativity scene (the birth of Jesus). Other children laughed when he laid them by the manger as an offering, but they fell silent when a brilliant red, star-shaped flower appeared on each branch.

Processions which enact Joseph and Mary's search for somewhere to stay in Bethlehem on the night Jesus was born begin nine days before Christmas, because Mary and Joseph's journey from Nazareth to Bethlehem took nine days. People form two groups: pilgrims and innkeepers. The pilgrims trudge from house to house asking for shelter. The innkeepers turn them away until they reach the house in which an altar and Nativity scene have been set up. They go in with great rejoicing, a traditional prayer is spoken, and the party begins.

Sweden

The "Yule log" comes from Scandinavia. Traditions concerned with warmth and light arose because of the long, dark, cold winters. "Yule" comes from the name of an ancient winter festival lasting 12 days. It was traditionally a time when fortunes for the coming year were determined and when the dead were thought to walk the earth.

Originally an entire tree was brought into the house with great ceremony. The bottom of the trunk was set into the hearth so that the rest of the tree stuck out into the room. It was burned until 6 January (the end of Yule).

A thousand years ago in Sweden, the King declared that Christmas would last a month, from the Feast of Saint Lucia (13 December) until Saint Knut's Day (13 January). Lucia was a 4th-century Sicilian saint and martyr who took food to Christians hiding from persecution in dark underground tunnels. To light the way she wore a wreath of candles on her head. She was discovered and killed. It is not known why she came to be revered in Sweden. Schools, businesses and communities sponsor processions of girls wearing white dresses and wreaths of candles; carols are sung and the Queen of Light is thanked for bringing hope at the darkest time of the year.

On Christmas Eve a Christmas gnome emerges from his home under the floor of the house or the barn. He brings a sack of gifts.

Nicaragua

In Nicaragua, Christmas begins on 7 December with *La Griteria* (The Calling), when groups of people call at each house in the neighbourhood singing joyful hymns to the Virgin Mary. The singers are given sweets and other small gifts. A giant doll, *La Gigantona* (The Female Giant), a symbol of Mary, is paraded dancing through the streets to the accompaniment of drums.

Japan

Christmas became popular in Japan at the beginning of the 20th century because of the Christmas products made there for other countries. It is a non-religious holiday devoted to children, and is celebrated mainly in cities.

Tinsel and lights are hung in dance halls, cafés and pinball parlours. Trees are decorated with small toys, dolls, gold paper fans and lanterns, wind chimes, candles and paper ornaments including origami swans.

Japanese children call Santa "Santa Kuroshu". He is believed to have eyes in the back of his head – to watch the children all year long!

Jamaica

On Christmas morning, processions of *jonkonoo* (masked dancing men) parade down the streets, beating drums to herald Christmas Day.

Ghana

In Ghana, Christmas celebrations go on for eight days. Children are given new clothes and other gifts. Bells ring all morning to call people to church.

The main dish for Christmas Day dinner is usually made from a fowl, goat or sheep. Yams and a soup made of meat and eggs are served.

In most towns, groups of children go from house to house, singing or chanting and blowing home-made trumpets throughout the eight days.

Iceland

Icelandic tradition has thirteen *Jolasveinar* (Christmas elves). *Jolasveinar* first appeared in the 17th century – the sons of the ogres *Gryla* and *Leppaludi*, who themselves had appeared in the 13th century and were said to have stolen and eaten naughty children.

The *Jolasveinar* live in mountains and start to arrive in towns, one a day, thirteen days before Christmas Eve, with the last one arriving that morning. As their names suggest, the *Jolasveinar* are playful imps who steal the seasonal food and play tricks: Door Slammer awakens sleepers by slamming doors; Candle Beggar snatches candles; and Meat Hooker tries to run off with the roast.

They also leave presents for children (in shoes the children have left on the windowsill the night before). If any children have been naughty, they leave a potato or some other reminder to be good. The elves start departing for home on Christmas Day, with the last one departing on Twelfth Night (6 January).

1 In which country do Christmas celebrations begin the earliest?

_____

1

On what date do they begin?

_____

1

2 In which country is Santa Claus said to have "eyes in the back of his head"?

_____

1

How are they useful?

_____

_____

_____

_____

1

3 Which country's Christmas celebrations have arisen because of the weather or climate there?

_____

1

4 Give three examples of Christmas celebrations which are based on legends not connected with the Nativity.

_____

_____

_____

_____

_____

3

TOTAL

8

5   What is the main similarity between Christmas celebrations in Sweden and Iceland?

1

_____

_____

_____

6   Japan is not a Christian country. What made the Japanese begin to celebrate Christmas?

1

_____

_____

_____

7   In which two countries are children likely to make sure they behave themselves as Christmas approaches?

1

_____

_____

Explain your answer.

2

_____

_____

_____

_____

_____

TOTAL

5

8   How has the writer organised the text to help readers to find facts about Christmas in any of the countries?

_____

_____

2

9   What type of text is the passage about "Christmas Celebrations"? Tick the correct answer.

argument	non-chronological report	persuasion	recount

1

How can you tell? (Think about features of the text, such as style of language, tense, person, the way in which points are organised.)

_____

_____

_____

4

TOTAL

7

Christmas Eve

From Her Benny by Silas Hocking

This book is set in Liverpool in the 1870s. Benny is ten and Nelly is nine years old. They make a living by selling matches. Benny also carries people's bags to and from the ferry-boats.

On Christmas Eve Benny took his sister through St John's Market, and highly delighted they were with what they saw. The thousands of geese, turkeys and pheasants, the loads of vegetables, the heaps of oranges and apples, the pyramids of every other conceivable kind of fruit, the stalls of sweetmeats, the tons of toffee, and the crowds of well-dressed people all bent upon buying something, were sources of infinite pleasure to the children. There was only one drawback to their happiness – they did not know how to lay out the sixpence they had brought with them to spend. If there had been less variety there would have been less difficulty; but, as it was, Benny felt as if he would never be able to decide what to buy. However, they agreed at last to lay out twopence for two slices of bread and ham, for they were both rather hungry; and then they spent the other fourpence on apples, oranges and toffee and, on the whole, felt very well satisfied with the result of their outlay.

It was rather later than usual when they got home, but old Betty knew where they had gone and, as it was Christmas Eve, she had got a bigger fire in than usual and had also got them a cup of hot cocoa each and some bunloaf to eat with it.

"By golly!" said Benny, as he munched the cake, "I do wish folks 'ud 'ave Christmas ev'ry week."

"You are a curious boy," said the old woman, looking up with a smile on her wrinkled face.

"Is I, Granny? I specks it's in my blood, as the chap said o' his timber leg."

The old woman had told them on the first evening of their arrival, when they had seemed at a loss what name to give her, to call her "Granny"; and no name could have been more appropriate, or have come more readily to the children's lips.

"But could folks 'ave Christmas any oftener if they wished to?" asked little Nell.

"Of course they could, Nell," burst out Benny. "You dunna seem to know what folks make Christmas for."

"An' I thinks you dunno either, Benny."

"Don't I, though?" he said, putting on an air of importance. "It's made to give folks the chance of doing a lot o' feeding; didn't yer see all the gooses an' other nice things in the market that folks is going to polish off tomorrow?"

"I dunna think it was made purpose for that. Wur it now, Granny?"

Thus appealed to, the old woman, who had listened with an amused smile on her face, answered, "No, my child. It's called Christmas because it is the birthday of Christ."

"Who's he?" said Benny, looking up, while Nelly's eyes echoed the enquiry.

"Don't you know – ain't you never heerd?" said the old woman in a tone of surprise.

"Nay," said Benny, "nuthin' sense."

"Poor little dears! I didn't know as how you was so ignorant, or I should have told you before." And the old woman looked as if she did not know where or how to begin to tell the children the wonderful story, and for a considerable time remained silent. At length she said, "I'll read it to 'ee out o' the Book; mebbe you'll understand it better that way nor any way else."

And, taking down from a shelf her big and much-worn Bible, she opened it and began to read:

"Now when Jesus was born in Bethlehem of Judea …" And slowly the old woman read on until she reached the end of the chapter, while the children listened with wide and wondering eyes. To Nelly the words seemed like a revelation, responding to the deepest feeling in her nature, and awakening thoughts within her that were too big for utterance. Benny, however, could see nothing particularly interesting in the narrative itself. But the art of reading was to him a mystery past all comprehension. How Granny could see that story upon the pages of her Bible was altogether beyond his grasp. At length, after scratching his head vigorously for some time, he burst out:

"By jabbers! I's got it at last! Jimmy Jones squeeze me if I ain't! It's the specks that does it!"

"Does what?" said Nelly.

"Why, the story bizness, to be sure. Let me look at the book through your specks, shall I, Granny?"

"Ay, if you like, Benny." And the next minute he was looking at the Bible with Granny's spectacles astride his nose and an expression of disappointment upon his face.

"Golly! I's sold!" was his exclamation. "But this are a poser, and no mistake."

"What's such a poser?" said Granny.

"Why, how yer find the story in the book; for I can see nowt."

Tick the correct answer for questions 1 to 6.

1   In which city do Nelly and Benny live?

| London | we are not told | Manchester | Liverpool |

2   Who was old Betty?

| the children's grandmother | the person they lived with | their mother | their neighbour |

3   What impressed Benny most about Christmas?

| the food | it was Christ's birthday | the snow | the money people spent |

4   What surprised old Betty?

| the amount of food the children ate | they had money to spend | they were late coming home | they didn't know who Christ was |

5   Why was Betty silent for quite a long time?

| she didn't know how or where to begin telling them the story of Christ | she was speechless at their ignorance | the children were arguing about what Christmas was for | she was day-dreaming |

6   What does Benny mean by "polish off"?

| eat | clean | tidy up | kill |

1

1

1

1

1

1

TOTAL

6

7 Do you think the children go to school?

_____

1

How can you tell?

_____

_____

1

8 List three different exclamations of surprise used by Benny.

_____

_____

_____

3

9 How can you tell that this book was written in Victorian times? Give three pieces of evidence from the passage.

_____

_____

_____

_____

3

10 How does the writer help readers to "hear" the way in which Nelly and Benny speak?

_____

_____

2

Give four examples.

_____

_____

4

TOTAL

14

4

11 List four dialect words (other than exclamations) which the characters use, and their meanings.

_____

_____

_____

_____

1

12 What was the atmosphere of St John's Market like?

_____

1

How does the author create this atmosphere?

_____

_____

_____

3

13 Give three examples of alliteration in the description of the market.

_____

_____

_____

1

14 At the end of the passage, what did Benny mean by "this are a poser"?

_____

_____

TOTAL

10

15 At the end of the passage, what puzzled Benny?

_____

1

How did he explain it?

_____

1

16 What can you tell about the narrator's religious beliefs?

_____

1

How can you tell?

_____

_____

4

_____

_____

_____

_____

TOTAL

7

The First Christmas

It never snows at Christmas in that dry and dusty land.

Instead of freezing blizzards, there are palms and drifting
    sands,

and years ago a stable and a most unusual star

and three wise men who followed it, by camel, not by car,

while, sleepy on the quiet hills, a shepherd gave a cry.

He'd seen a crowd of angels in the silent starlit sky.

In the stable, ox and ass stood very still and calm

and gazed upon the baby, safe and snug, in Mary's arms.

And Joseph, lost in shadows, face lit by an oil lamp's glow

stood wondering, that first Christmas Day, two thousand
    years ago.

Marian Swinger

1 What is the climate like in the land of the first Christmas?

| dry and hot | cold and wet | dry and cold | hot and wet |

1

2 What kind of plant grows there?

_____

1

3 How did the wise men travel?

_____

1

4 How long ago was the first Christmas?

_____

1

5 Give an example of half rhyme from the poem.

_____

1

6 Which word best describes the atmosphere of the poem?

| exciting | calm | scary | gloomy |

1

Write two words or phrases that help to create this atmosphere

_____

2

TOTAL

8

1

2

3

4

7 Write an example of alliteration that includes three words.

_____

_____

What mood or atmosphere does this repeated sound create?

_____

_____

8 Describe the rhyme pattern of the poem.

_____

_____

9 What is the poet saying about Christmas now and the first Christmas?

_____

_____

What evidence can you find in the poem for this?

_____

_____

_____

TOTAL

10

This test helps you to gain an insight into your child's ability to write independently and to communicate meaning to the reader using the conventions of punctuation, spelling and handwriting.

In the Optional Tests at Key Stage 2 children's writing is assessed through two Writing Tests:

- a Longer Writing Test (45 minutes)
- a Shorter Writing Test (20 minutes).

Children should be allowed time to plan their writing for both tests, which they should not do one after the other.

The **Longer Test** is assessed for: **Sentence structure and punctuation, Text structure and organisation** and **Composition and effect**. The **Shorter Test** is assessed for **Sentence structure, punctuation and text organisation** and **Composition and effect**.

Sentence structure and punctuation focuses on the use of variation of types of sentences, clarity, purpose and effect, and on grammatical accuracy and punctuation.

Text structure and organisation focuses on organising and presenting whole texts effectively, sequencing and structuring information, ideas and events, constructing paragraphs and using cohesion within and between paragraphs.

Composition and effect focuses on imaginative, interesting and thoughtful writing; writing a text which is suitable for its purpose and for the reader; and organising and presenting a text effectively.

Grammar, **punctuation** and **spelling** are assessed in a separate test.

The mark schemes each year are specific to the tests; new level thresholds are set for each year's tests to ensure that standards are maintained each year.

Assessment of children's attainment in National Tests depends on the judgement of professionals who use a more precise numerical marking system. For the purposes of this book, a simplified system of marking is used based on Content (Composition and effect) and Grammar and structure (Sentence structure, Punctuation and Text organisation).

Guidelines to National Curriculum Levels are provided on pages 80 and 104. These should be regarded as a rough guide only.

Your child should first have read the passages in the Reading Tests.

Allow **45 minutes** for the **Longer (Fiction)** Writing Test and **20 minutes** for the **Shorter (Non-fiction)** Writing Test.

There are no definitive answers, but criteria are given on page 78 to help you assess your child's National Curriculum Level.

FOR FICTION: Introduce the planning sheet and read the starting point aloud. Discuss the headings on the sheet. Emphasise the importance of:

- writing a whole story and not just part of it;
- planning the story;
- thinking of a good opening to make the reader want to read on;
- keeping the reader interested;
- introducing the setting, the main character and the plot early in the story;
- helping the reader to get to know the characters;
- thinking of a good ending, rather than stopping abruptly.

FOR NON-FICTION: Read the instructions and ask your child if he or she thinks everyone should have Christmas Day off work. Ask him or her to consider the reasons for this opinion and to write them on the chart in the appropriate place.

Discuss the other headings on the chart and emphasise the importance of:

- introducing the argument to orientate the readers
- supporting opinions with evidence
- being prepared for arguments against it
- summarising the argument at the end (the conclusion).

You must not tell your child what to write!

For both tasks, point out that grammar, spelling and punctuation are important.

Remind your child to think about punctuation and how it helps the reader to make sense of what is written.

If your child finishes before the allotted time is up, encourage him or her to read through what he or she has written to look for anything which can be improved and to check grammar, spelling and punctuation.

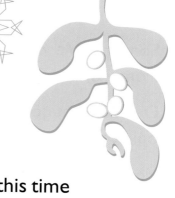

Making sense of Christmas

Read the extract from *Her Benny* and the poem "The First Christmas". Write a story from the point of view of a visitor from another planet who has observed people celebrating Christmas and is trying to make sense of what he or she observes.

You have 45 minutes. Spend about 10 to 15 minutes of this time planning what you will write. Use the planning guidelines below.

Title

Setting

Where does the story take place?

When does it take place?

Characters

Name them and make notes about their personal qualities and characteristics.

Who is the main character or the narrator?

Who are the other characters?

Opening

Think of an opening which sets the scene and interests the reader.

Middle

Plan this section in paragraphs: what is each paragraph about?

Ending

How does the story end?

Have you forgotten anything?

Christmas – a holiday for everyone?

Some people work on Christmas Day. Should everyone be given a holiday from work at Christmas?

Decide what your opinion is, and why, and write an argument to support your opinion.

You have 20 minutes. Spend about 5 to 10 minutes planning what you will write. Use the planning sheet below.

Write an introduction, three main paragraphs and a conclusion.

Write the evidence to support your opinion. Also think of the arguments other people might make against this. Write some counter-arguments against these.

I think that		
Reasons	Arguments against	Counter-arguments
Summary		

Decide in which person to write (first – I, me, we, us – or third – he, him, she, her, they), how formal or informal your writing should be and whether it should be mainly active or passive ("they do this" or "this is done").

Make a list of useful connective words for an argument.
Use the chart to help you to plan each paragraph.
Think of a suitable introduction and conclusion (one sentence each).

Grammar, Punctuation and Spelling Test 1

The test will assess children's abilities in the following technical aspects of English:

- grammar
- punctuation
- spelling
- vocabulary.

The test will assess Levels 3–5 of the current English curriculum. A separate Level 6 test will be available for schools that wish to enter children who are expected to be working above Level 5 at the time of the test.

The current English writing test assesses technical English skills through writing composition. This test uses closed response and short response questions to assess these elements of the programme of study.

Allow 40 minutes for each Grammar, Punctuation and Spelling test.

1 Complete the chart with the correct versions of the verbs.

Present	Past	Future
Today I ...	Yesterday I ...	Tomorrow I will ...
jump		
drink		
think	thought	
buy		
make		
break		
am		be

6

2 Complete the chart to make opposites.

Word	Add the negative prefix	New word
possible	im	impossible
behave		
appear		
clean		
legible		
approve		

5

3 Add the suffix 'ing' to these words. Complete the chart.

Root word	Add 'ing'
slide	
beg	
eat	
sit	

4

TOTAL

15

74

4 Write the speech marks in the correct places in these sentences.

5

Dirt won't do any harm anyway, I sighed.

You are just cheeky, Dad declared.

I just dug up that plant, I said.

Look out! he screamed.

Oops! It's just another weed really, Dad, I insisted, as I ran out of the garden.

5 This passage is full of repetition.

- Change some of the nouns for pronouns, such as 'he', to avoid the repetition and to make it sound better.

3

- Write out the new passage below.

Fred the monster was given a new rocket for his birthday. Fred the monster also got a new Zapper and two robots to help him. Fred wanted to play with his new toys. The first thing Fred did was to charge up the robot but the robot was broken. Fred went to the other robot and this time the robot sprang into life. Fred rushed to the office to tell his father. Fred's father was not happy to see him as Fred's father was very busy. Just then Fred's robot came walking into the room. Fred's father laughed so much that Fred's father fell off his chair.

Fred the monster was given a new rocket for his birthday. He also got …

_____

_____

_____

_____

_____

_____

_____

TOTAL

8

75

5

6 Write 'ie' or 'ei' in these words.

pr_ _st

dec_ _t

rec_ _pt

rel_ _f

ch_ _f

4

7 Complete the chart to change adjectives to nouns.

Adjective	Noun
warm	warmth
young	
long	
strong	
beautiful	

5

8 Complete the examples, writing the apostrophe in the correct place.

the whiskers of the cat

the cat's whiskers

a hat of a lady

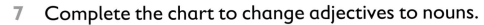

the leaves of a tree

the bananas of all the monkeys

the bottles of two babies

some money of my dad

TOTAL

14

Question number	Answer	Mark
NON-FICTION		
1	Nicaragua. 7 December.	2
2	Japan.	1
	To keep an eye on children.	1
3	Sweden.	1
4	The Yule log and St Lucia's Day in Sweden and the *Jolasveinar* in Iceland.	3
5	Gnomes or elves bring gifts.	1
6	They made Christmas products for other countries.	1
7	Iceland and Japan.	1
	In Iceland, the elves leave presents only for children who have been good; if they have been naughty the elves leave a potato or some other reminder to behave themselves. In Japan, Santa watches what they are doing all through the year.	2
8	The names of the countries are used as headings for sections of the text.	2
9	Non-chronological report.	1
	It is mainly in the present tense. It is in the third person. Points or information are grouped into sections and not in chronological order.	4
FICTION		
1	Liverpool	1
2	the person they lived with	1
3	the food	1
4	they didn't know who Christ was	1
5	she didn't know how or where to begin telling them the story of Christ	1
6	eat	1
7	No.	1
	They cannot read *or* they have never heard the story of the Nativity.	1
8	By golly! By jabbers! Golly! I's sold!	1 for each. Max 3
9	The introduction says that it was set in the 1870s. It cost only two pence for two slices of bread and ham and four pence for apples, oranges and toffee.	3
10	He changes the spellings of the words and sometimes he also joins two words together. Examples: 'ud (would), 'ave (have), ev'ry (every), dunna (do not), dunno (do not know), nuthin' (nothing).	2 4
11	I specks (I expect), specks (glasses/spectacles), dunna (do not/don't), polish off (eat), 'ee (you), ain't (are not/have not), dunno (don't know), nowt (nothing)	4 for four, 1 for one to three
12	busy and full of Christmas foods	1
	"Crowds of people" and lists of the things the children see, with words which give the impression of large amounts, like thousands, heaps, tons and loads.	1
13	stalls of sweetmeats, tons of toffee, bent upon buying	3 for all three, 1 for one or two
14	"This is a puzzle" (or "this is strange" or a similar answer)	1
15	He wondered how old Betty could see the story on the pages of the Bible.	1
	He thought her glasses did it.	1
16	He is a Christian.	1
	He calls the story of Christ "the wonderful story". The story suggests that the children ought to know about it.	4 for both observations, 1 for one of them
POETRY		
1	dry and hot	1
2	palms	1
3	by camel	1
4	two thousand years	1
5	land/sands or calm/arms	1
6	calm	1
	any two from the following: sleepy, quiet silent, still and calm, safe and snug	2 (one mark for each example)

Question number	Answer	Mark
7	silent starlit sky calm and quiet	1 2
8	rhyming couplets (or pairs of rhyming lines)	3
9	It was different from the modern Christmas: much calmer and quieter, everything was much slower and there was no snow. Evidence: "dry and dusty", "instead of freezing blizzards, there are palms and drifting sands", "by camel, not by car", "sleepy on the quiet hills", "silent starlit sky", "very still and calm" (or a similar answer).	4

- Marks: out of 75. Divide by two thirds to achieve a mark out of 50.

Answers

Writing Test 1

The following criteria provide guidelines to help you gain an idea of your child's Writing Level. A more precise numerical marking system is used by professional markers for marking National Tests. Each level assumes that the criteria for the previous level have been met. Marks are out of 30.

Content (composition and effect)	Level
Is the writing in the correct form (for example, in an appropriate layout and in the correct person and tense)? Is fiction writing imaginative? Is non-fiction writing clear and does it have a logical structure?	Level 3
Is there an attempt to interest the reader? Is the style or viewpoint maintained throughout most of the writing? Are the criteria suggested on the planning sheet met?	Level 4
Is the tone of the writing maintained throughout? Is the language expressive and effective? Are the vocabulary and language appropriate for the purpose of the writing (for example, the use of technical or subject-based language, metaphors, similes or comparisons)? Are they suitable for the readers?	Level 5
Grammar and structure (sentence structure, punctuation and text organisation)	
Are the ideas presented in sequence, with full stops, capital letters, question marks and commas usually used correctly? Is a greater range of connective words and phrases used (for example, next, afterwards, so)?	Level 3
Are some of the sentences long, with correctly-used connective words and phrases (for example, meanwhile, however, which, that, who)? Are conditionals, such as if or because, used? Do some sentences contain more than one verb or include commas, semi-colons, exclamation marks or speech marks? Are the tense and person consistent throughout? Does the structure of the text add to its effect?	Level 4
Are commas and speech marks used correctly throughout? Is a range of connective words and phrases used? Is a range of punctuation marks used correctly, including brackets or dashes and colons to separate parts of a sentence? Is the length of the sentences varied to express meaning? Are passive or active verbs used appropriately?	Level 5

Level	Mark range
2	0–5
3	6–11
4	12–17
5	18–30

Question number	Answer	Mark
1	jump – jumped – jump drink – drank – drink think – thought – think buy – bought – buy make – made – make break – broke – break am – was – be	Half a mark for each correct answer in the chart/out of 6
2	behave – misbehave appear – disappear clean – unclean legible – illegible approve – disapprove	Half a mark for each correct answer in the chart/out of 5
3	sliding; begging; eating; sitting	One mark for each correct spelling/out of 4
4	"Dirt won't do any harm anyway," I sighed. "You are just cheeky," Dad declared. "I just dug up that plant," I said. "Look out!" he screamed. "Oops! It's just another weed really, Dad," I insisted, as I ran out of the garden.	One mark for each correct sentence with speech marks placed appropriately/out of 5
5	He also got a new Zapper and two robots to help him. He wanted to play with his new toys. The first thing Fred did was to charge up the robot but it was broken. He went to the other robot and this time the robot sprang into life. He rushed to the office to tell his father. His father was not happy to see him as he was very busy. Just then Fred's robot came walking into the room. Fred's father laughed so much that he fell off his chair.	Mark proportionally. The questions tests that the child can use pronouns appropriately to avoid repetition/out of 6
6	priest; deceit; receipt; relief; chief	One mark for each correct spelling/out of 5
7	youth; length; strength; beauty	One mark for each correct answer/out of 4
8	a lady's hat; a tree's leaves; my dad's money; two babies' bottles; the monkeys' bananas	One mark for each correct answer/out of 5
Total: divide by 2 so score is out of 20		

Assessment of children's attainment in National Curriculum tests depends upon the judgement of professionals. For the purposes of this book, a simplified system of marking is used. Guidelines to National Curriculum levels provided should be regarded as a rough guide only.

Use the conversion tables below to gain an idea of your child's National Curriculum Level.

English – reading		English – writing		English – grammar, punctuation and spelling		English – overall	
Level	Mark range	Level	Mark range	Level	Mark range	Level	Mark range
N	0–10	N	0–5	N	0–3	N	0–19
3	11–17	3	6–11	3	4–9	2	20–22
4	18–33	4	12–17	4	10–15	3	23–40
5	34–50	5	18–30	5	16–20	4	41–69
						5	70–100

Enter your child's results below:

English – reading	English – writing	English – grammar, punctuation and spelling	English – overall
Mark	Mark	Mark	Mark

Estimated National Curriculum Level: _____

The Reading Test at Key Stage 2 comprises a variety of texts – non-fiction, fiction and poetry – to test reading strategies across a range of genres. There will normally be a common theme.

The questions require four different kinds of answers:

- Short words or phrases (one mark for each correct response).

- Longer answers (one or two sentences) which require more understanding of the text (two marks).

- Detailed explanations of opinion (up to three marks).

- Multiple choice (one mark).

Although some questions will have a "right answer", all children will express their responses in a different way. Marking guidelines are given on pages 100–101 and an indication of National Curriculum Levels on page 104.

Allow 15 minutes for reading all three passages (when no writing is allowed) and 45 minutes for answering the questions.

Setting the test

1. Encourage your child to read the introduction below and each passage carefully.

2. Point out the different types of questions: those which give a choice of answers to tick or circle, and those which need a written answer. Written answers need not be complete sentences. Some written answers are worth three or more marks if detail or examples are required.

3. Do not help your child to read the text, although you may help with the spelling of the answers.

4. Point out that your child may rub out or alter any mistakes.

5. Tell your child:

- to find the answers in the text, rather than guessing;
- to tick or circle only one box in multiple choice questions;
- to try to answer every question;
- to leave any questions he or she cannot answer and go back to them at the end;
- to re-read the text to find the answers.

Other worlds

Contents

Non-fiction: **The Inuit**

Fiction: **Little House in the Big Woods**

Poetry: **The Sioux Indians**

You will look at aspects of living in places and times very different from your own. The world and the daily activities which are described may seem very different, and the passages examine this and other themes. The passages are:

- from an information text about the Inuit people;
- from a novel set in the "Wild West' past;
- from a ballad about North American Indians.

You have **15 minutes** to read through these passages and **45 minutes** to answer the questions.

The Inuit

This passage is adapted from a book written more than 30 years ago. At that time, the Inuit people had little contact with the rest of the world. Nowadays, they have many of the modern things we have.

The Inuit people (formerly known as Eskimos) live in the northernmost margin of the New World, along the coasts of the Arctic Ocean, above the line where the trees will grow.

They have learned how to live in a world where:
- in the farthest north there are four months when the sun does not rise above the horizon;
- there are only two months when the sun shines all day round and there are no frosts.

This means that the seas are often frozen and the waterways are blocked.

During most of the year the Inuit people live in danger:
- of being caught in blizzards;
- of being marooned on breaking ice at sea;
- of starving to death when the weather keeps the hunters at home.

How does this affect their lives?
- They cannot afford to look after their old people in the ways in which we do. The old people themselves ask to be allowed to die rather than become a burden on the group.
- The dogs which pull their sledges are precious to them. However, in times of real hardship, the Inuit people have to choose between starving or eating their dogs.
- Some scientists believe that no other groups of people have to experience such a hard life, but they are a cheerful and hospitable people.

How do they spend their time?
Coming into an ice-house after a day's hunting, in from the cold and the dark, you might find half the people of the settlement crowded in the warmth. Small babies and puppies might be playing and crawling around; adults might be playing games with tiny carved ivory animals for dice, trying out new tongue-twisters on one another or making string figures. There will be much laughter, between eating meat and listening to a storyteller.

Facts about the Inuit
- Even though it is often hard work to get enough to eat, they welcome visitors.
- Travelling is dangerous in the remote parts of Alaska, but Inuit people travel a great deal, often staying away for years.
- They hunt seals, walruses, bears and whales.
- Some still live in ice-houses – traditional "igloos".

Tick the correct answer in each of questions 1 to 4.

1 The Inuit people were once known as:

| Eskimos | New World | Arctic | Northern-most margin |

1

2 Where they live:

| there are no frosts | the sun shines all the time | the sun does not shine for four months | the horizon does not rise for four months |

1

3 We know the Inuit live in a snowy climate because it says:

| they get marooned | they starve to death | they get caught in blizzards | they have to stay at home all the time |

1

4 The animal which is most precious to the Inuit is:

| the dog | the walrus | the whale | the bear |

1

TOTAL

4

5 Write down TWO things which, according to the passage, occur because there are long periods without sunlight.

1

_____

_____

_____

_____

6 These questions are about the ways in which information is presented.

a Why have these words been made to stand out?

b Why are these words smaller and in *italic* print?

3

c Why is this text in a separate box?

a _____

b _____

c _____

_____

TOTAL

4

84

7 Which TWO of the following are the purposes of this extract? Tick the correct boxes.

	to persuade the reader to protect the Inuit people
	to inform the reader about the Inuit people
	to provide instructions on how to reach the Inuit people
	to write a story about the Inuit people
	to explain some interesting things about the Inuit people

1

8 Imagine you go into an Inuit house. Write FOUR things you might see happening.

_____

_____

_____

_____

2

9 Which one do you find most interesting, and why?

_____

_____

_____

_____

2

10 Explain FOUR ways in which the last paragraph of the passage supports what the writer has said about the Inuit people being cheerful and hospitable.

_____

_____

_____

_____

_____

_____

_____

4

TOTAL

9

85

Little House in the Big Woods

The story is set in the pioneering days of the Wild West in the mid nineteenth century.

Laura and Mary had never seen a town. They had never seen a store. They had never seen even two houses standing together. But they knew that in a town there were many houses, and a store full of candy and calico and other wonderful things – powder, and shot, and salt, and store sugar.

They knew that Pa would trade his furs to the storekeeper for beautiful things from the town, and all day they were expecting the presents he would bring them. When the sun sank low above the treetops and no more drops fell from the tips of the icicles they began to watch eagerly for Pa.

The sun sank out of sight, the woods grew dark, and he did not come. Ma started supper and set the table, but he did not come. It was time to do the chores, and still he had not come.

Ma said that Laura might come with her while she milked the cow. Laura could carry the lantern.

So Laura put on her coat and Ma buttoned it up. And Laura put her hands into the red mittens that hung by a red yarn string around her neck, while Ma lighted the candle in the lantern.

Laura was proud to be helping Ma with the milking, and she carried the lantern very carefully. Its sides were of tin, with places cut in them for the candle-light to shine through.

When Laura walked behind Ma on the path to the barn, the little bits of candle-light from the lantern leaped all around her on the snow. The night was not yet quite dark. The woods were dark, but there was a grey light on the snowy path, and in the sky there were a few faint stars. The stars did not look as warm and bright as the little lights that came from the lantern.

Laura was surprised to see the dark shape of Sukey, the brown cow, standing at the barnyard gate. Ma was surprised, too.

It was too early in the spring for Sukey to be let out in the Big Woods to eat grass. She lived in the barn. But sometimes on warm days Pa left the door of her stall open so she could come into the barnyard. Now Ma and Laura saw her behind the bars, waiting for them.

Ma went up to the gate, and pushed against it to open it. But it did not open very far, because there was Sukey, standing against it. Ma said:
"Sukey, get over!" She reached across the gate and slapped Sukey's shoulder.

Just then one of the dancing bits of light from the lantern jumped between the bars of the gate, and Laura saw long, shaggy, black fur, and two little, glittering eyes. Sukey had thin, short, brown fur. Sukey had large, gentle eyes.

Ma said, "Laura, walk back to the house."

So Laura turned around and began to walk towards the house. Ma came behind her. When they had gone part way, Ma snatched her up, lantern and all, and ran. Ma ran with her into the house, and slammed the door.

Then Laura said, "Ma, was it a bear?"

Tick the correct answer in each of questions 1 to 4.

1   You can tell Laura and Mary lived in the countryside in the time of the Wild West because the writer says that they had never seen:

candy and calico	a town or a store	powder and shot	salt and store sugar

2   The father was a trader in:

powder	candy	furs	salt

3   When they went to milk the cow, Laura carried:

her mittens	a milk churn	a gun	the lantern

4   Laura's mittens were:

red	not attached to string	warm	full of holes

1

1

1

1

TOTAL

4

5 Which words and phrases from the passage show that the family was worried about their father when he did not arrive on time?

_____

_____

1

6 Find two pieces of evidence from the passage to show that Laura was a very young child.

_____

_____

_____

1

7 The passage creates a picture of the world of Laura and her family. Complete the chart with descriptive words and phrases from the extract.

4

Picture	How it is described in the passage
Candle-light from the lantern in the snow	
The light on the snowy path in the woods	
The stars in the sky	
The bear	

8 Put these events from the extract in the correct order.
Write numbers 1 to 5 in the boxes to show the order.

	Laura helps her mother feed Sukey but they are surprised to find her waiting for them.
	The children wait at home for their father to arrive with gifts for them.
	Laura's mother does not panic. She tells her to walk back to the house ignoring what she has seen.
	He does not arrive so they start to do their daily chores.
6	As they get close to the house her mother panics, picks her up and runs, to reach the safety of the house.
	In the lantern light Laura sees shaggy fur and glittering eyes – a bear is close by.

9 In your own words, describe how Laura felt at various parts of the story.

When she was waiting for her father.

When he did not turn up.

When she went with her mother to milk the cow.

When she saw the bear.

Find quotations to prove your points.

_____

_____

_____

_____

_____

_____

TOTAL

9

The Sioux Indians

This is a ballad about North American Indians.

I'll sing you a song and it'll be a sad one,
Of trials and troubles and how first begun,
We left our dear kindred, our friends and our home,
Across the wild deserts and mountains we roam. *(twice)*

We crossed the Missouri and joined a large train,
Which bore us o'er mountains and valleys and plains,
And often of an evening out hunting we'd go
To shoot the fleet antelope and the wild buffalo. *(twice)*

We heard of Sioux Indians all out on the plains,
A-killing poor drivers and burning their trains,
A-killing poor drivers with arrows and bows,
When captured by Indians, no mercy they'd show. *(twice)*

We travelled three weeks till we came to the Platte,
We set up our camp at the head of the flat,
We spread down our blankets on the green grassy ground,
While our mules and our horses were grazing around. *(twice)*

While taking refreshment we heard a low yell,
The whoop of Sioux Indians coming out of the dell,
We sprang to our rifles with a flash in each eye,
'Boys,' said our brave leader, 'we'll fight till we die.' *(twice)*

They made a bold dash and come near to our train,
The arrows fell round us like showers of rain,
But with our long rifles we fed them hot lead,
Till many a brave warrior around us lay dead. *(twice)*

Tick the correct answer in each of questions 1 to 3.

1   We are told that the poem is going to be:

| a funny one | a sad one | a long one | a friendly one |

½

2   The people in the poem left home and travelled across:

| only deserts | only mountains | deserts and mountains | the jungle |

½

3   How long had they been travelling before they were attacked by the Sioux Indians?

| three weeks | three months | an evening | a week |

1

4   Find the old-fashioned words in the poem that mean the following.

Family: _____

Fast and agile: _____

1

5   Which of the following statements are true or false? Explain why.

Statement	True or false?	Explain why
The settlers travelling across America were travelling on a steam train.		
The Sioux Indians had a very bad reputation with the settlers.		
This poem is a ballad and was meant to be sung.		
They spent their time during the day hunting wild animals.		

4

TOTAL

7

4

6 The poet creates a picture by careful use of adjectives. Explain what the following adjectives tell you about what they are describing to create a picture in your mind:

Adjective	What it tells me
wild (deserts)	
green grassy (ground)	
bold (dash)	
brave (warrior)	

1

7 The poet uses very vivid words in the poem to help the description and the atmosphere.

a What does "whoop" add to the description of the Indian attack?

_____

b What does "sprang to our rifles" add to the description of the men's reaction?

_____

2

8 In your own words, describe the effect of the following in the poem.

a "The arrows fell round us like showers of rain". What is the simile describing? How are the two things similar? What impression does it give you about how many arrows were fired? How did they look to the writer? How did they fall to the ground?

_____

_____

b "we fed them hot lead". What is the metaphor describing? Was the lead really hot? What effect is the writer aiming for? What does it tell you about the ferocity of the fighting?

TOTAL

_____

_____

7

You will find more information about this test on page 69. Your child should first have read the passages in the Reading Test.

Allow **45 minutes** for the **Longer (Non-fiction)** Writing Test and **20 minutes** for the **Shorter (Fiction) Writing** Test.

There are no definitive answers, but criteria are given on page 102 to help you assess your child's National Curriculum Level.

FOR NON-FICTION: Discuss the points on the planning sheet. Emphasise the importance of:

- thinking up a good introduction to make the reader want to read on;
- keeping the reader interested;
- making the text easy for the reader to follow;
- thinking of a good ending so that the information does not just "tail off".

You must not tell your child what to write!

FOR FICTION: Introduce the planning sheet and read the starting point aloud. Discuss the headings on it. Emphasise the importance of:

- writing a whole story and not just part of it;
- planning the story;
- thinking of a good opening to make the reader want to read on;
- keeping the reader interested;
- introducing the setting, the main character and the plot early in the story;
- helping the reader to get to know the characters;
- thinking of a good ending, rather than stopping abruptly.

For both tasks, point out that grammar, spelling and punctuation are important.

Remind your child to think about punctuation and how it helps the reader to make sense of what is written.

If your child finishes writing before the allotted time is up, encourage him or her to read it through to look for anything which can be improved and to check grammar, spelling and punctuation.

Longer Writing Test 2 (Non-Fiction)

Planning Sheet

For or against hunting

Read the three extracts in the Reading Test and make notes about what each one says about people's reactions to wild animals. Suppose these wild animals were to be hunted.

Write a passage which gives your views about whether hunting wild animals should be banned.

You have 45 minutes. Spend about 10 to 15 minutes planning what you will write.

Use the planning guidelines below.

Decide in which person you should write ("I..." or "we..."), how formal or informal your writing should be, and whether it should be mainly active or passive ("we should do this" or "this should be done").

Make notes of any useful words or phrases.

Make notes of useful connective words or other words.

Plan the contents of each paragraph.

Think of arguments and details to prove your point.

Think of any arguments which someone might use against you.

Think of a suitable introduction and conclusion.

When I looked around, I was completely surrounded by animals ...

Continue the story in a way you think is appropriate.

Explain how this situation occurred.

You have 20 minutes. Spend about 5 minutes planning what you will write.

Use the planning guidelines below.

Title _____

Setting

Where does the story take place?

When does it take place?

Characters

Name them and make notes about their personal qualities and characteristics.

Who is the main character or the narrator?

Who are the other characters?

Opening

Develop an opening to set the scene and interest the reader.

Middle

Plan this section in paragraphs: what is each paragraph about?

Ending

How does the story end? Have you forgotten anything?

For an introduction to the Grammar, Punctuation and Spelling test, see page 73.

1 Underline the verb in each sentence.

a The swan glided across the lake.

b The mosquito darted in front of my eyes.

c The butterfly fluttered around the flower.

d The ducks waddled down the path.

e My cat stalked the mouse.

f The mouse scurried into the hole.

g The pony trotted into the farm.

h The snake slithered across the grass.

2 Write the plurals of these words. Careful – some of them are tricky!

a man _____   d mouse _____

b goose _____   e fish _____

c woman _____

3 Complete the chart to see how the spelling of the words is transformed.

Noun	Verb
action	to act
knee	
	to sparkle
freedom	
	to amuse
excitement	

4

5

5

TOTAL

14

96

4 A clause is a group of words containing a **verb** and a **subject**. It can be used as a whole sentence or as part of a sentence, e.g. 'They peep out slyly.'

- Add clauses beginning with **when** or **where** to these sentences.

   a The racing car went out of control _____

   _____

   b I will get a new car _____

   _____

   c I hope you can see _____

   _____

   d There was a huge snake in the grass _____

   _____

4

5 Complete the chart. Write out the correct versions using apostrophes.

4

Words in full	Shortened form with apostrophe
it is	it's
we are	
there is	
I will	
cannot	
he is	
shall not	
did not	
they have	

TOTAL

8

97

6 Add the suffix '-ly' to the words below. Write out the correct spellings.

friend   _____

near   _____

lucky   _____

happy   _____

safe   _____

thankful   _____

final   _____

simple   _____

7 Rewrite these sentences, putting the commas in the correct places.

a Cakes are made from flour milk butter and sugar.

_____

b Freda ordered a burger a large cola a big bag of fries and a chocolate cake before she was ill.

_____

_____

c Her sister is rude lazy silly and very good looking.

_____

d As a gift I bought chocolates ice-cream flowers and a CD.

_____

e In the box there were piles of books – old dirty dog-eared smelly and unwanted – worth a fortune.

_____

_____

4

5

TOTAL

9

98

8   Complete the chart.

Prefix	Examples of word using this prefix	What I think the prefix means from the words
semi	semicircle, semi-detached	half of something, a part of
photo		
tele		
bi		
circu		

4

9   The part of the sentence in A can be joined to a part of a sentence in B.

- Write out the correct sentences using a semi-colon (;).

A	B
He lifted the seat	the nights were getting shorter.
Fred loves Chinese food	the big spider crawled out.
It was Autumn	they had not had time for a chat before.
I had lost the key	Sophie likes Indian food.
Mum and Dad talked all through the holiday	I would be in trouble.

5

_____

_____

_____

_____

_____

_____

_____

_____

_____

_____

TOTAL

9

Answers

Reading Test 2

Question number	Answer	Mark	Parent's notes and additional information
NON-FICTION			
1	Eskimos	1	
2	the sun does not shine for four months	1	
3	they get caught in blizzards	1	
4	the dog	1	
5	the seas freeze, the waterways become blocked	1	One half mark per correct answer.
6a	This is a main title.	1	
b	This is an introduction to tell the reader what is in that particular section. It is in *italics* so that it stands out as being different.	1	
c	The boxed text is used for interesting facts. They need to stand out as being different from the rest.	1	
7	To inform the reader about the Inuit people. To explain some interesting things about the Inuit people.	1	One half mark per correct answer.
8	Any four from: many people crowded inside; babies and puppies playing; adults playing with dice games; people trying out tongue-twisters (word games) with one another; making string figures; laughter; eating meat; listening to storytellers.	2	One half mark per correct answer.
9	Any answer, e.g. animals and children playing together may be considered unhygienic in our society.	2	Your child should show an ability to compare his or her experiences with those of the Inuit.
10	They all get on well together – even in a confined space. They all enjoy doing simple things, e.g. making string figures. There is laughter and game playing. Many activities are communal and involve people working together.	4	One mark per correct answer.
FICTION			
1	a town or a store	1	Explore the idea that the question asks only for what the writer says in the passage – nor what may be otherwise true through deduction.
2	furs	1	
3	the lantern	1	
4	red	1	Again, some of the other options may have been true but they were not stated in the passage.
5	Any one of: "… but he did not come". "… still he had not come".	1	The question asks for quotations, so be sure to provide these. You may wish to talk about the use of quotation marks.
6	Laura was allowed to carry the lantern. This was made to seem like a very important thing to do. She was proud to do this. Her mittens were on "a red yarn string around her neck", in case she lost them. The tone of the passage suggests a young child who did not really understand the seriousness of the situation. "Ma buttoned up her coat." (Laura couldn't do it for herself.)	1	One half mark per correct answer.

Question number	Answer	Mark	Parent's notes and additional information
7	Candle-light from the lantern in the snow: "leaped all around her on the snow". The light on the snowy path in the woods: "but there was a grey light on the snowy path". The stars in the sky: "a few faint stars. The stars did not look as warm and bright …" The bear: "long, shaggy, black fur, and two little, glittering eyes".	4	Again, the question asks for quotations, so be sure to provide these. You may wish to talk about the use of quotation marks.
8	The order in the chart is: 3, 1, 5, 2, 6, 4.	5	Use this question to discuss the structure of the story and how it builds tension.
9	When she was waiting for her father: she was excited at the thought of gifts from the store but she was also anxious when her father does not turn up on time. "wonderful things …"; "…but he did not come." When he did not turn up: she is anxious but as a young child she does not really understand the implications of this. "… and still he had not come." When she went with her mother to milk the cow: she was proud and excited to be helping her mother and holding the lantern. "Laura was proud to be helping Ma … carried the lantern very carefully …" She was "surprised to see the shape of Sukey." When she saw the bear: she is not afraid. She sees something and she knows that this creature is not the same as their cow. It is not until she sees her mother's panic and they get back to the safety of the house that she asks if it was a bear. "Ma, was it a bear?"	4	Note that the question asks for "own words" so this is important. It also asks for quotations to back up these points.
POETRY			
1	A sad one	½	Explore the idea that the question asks only for what the writer says in the passage – not what may be otherwise assumed through deduction.
2	Deserts and mountains	½	Again, the question is specific to the information in verse 1.
3	Three weeks	1	Verse 4 – they had travelled for three weeks and set up camp by the River Platte.
4	Family – kindred Fast and agile – fleet	1	This will need discussion as deduction from the context is necessary. Encourage the use of dictionaries.
5	False. The train referred to is a wagon train. It is obvious from the references to setting up camp and hunting that they will not have been travelling by steam train. It is also unlikely that there was any train track in undiscovered country. True. The Indians did have a bad reputation – "we heard of Sioux Indians …" True. The poem is a ballad – see line 1, "I'll sing you a song". Also there is a request for a refrain after each verse. False. The poem says that they hunted during "the evening". Naturally during the day, they will have been travelling.	4	Discussion about the meaning of words – some of which change over time – and what really happens in the poem may be necessary.
6	Wild – shows something of the troublesome journey the settlers had to face. It was wild because of the scenery as well as the threat of the Indians. Green grassy – shows their relief when they emerge from the desert to be finding somewhere so good to camp, and spend their night. Bold – shows something of the desperation of the Indian attackers. They were being brave and not considering their own safety, hence they were dangerous adversaries. Brave – this suggests something of admiration for the Indian fighters.	4	Identify adjectives and what they do – describe nouns. Discuss how the use of these describing words can add information about what the noun is like and also about how the writer feels.
7	"Whoop" is an onomatopoeic word. It makes the sound of the Indians as they attacked, so we can actually hear them. It also gives us a sense of the fear the men may have felt being attacked by such strange creatures. It makes the opponent seem more savage. The men "sprang" suggests the speed with which they responded to the attack. They were ready and they reacted appropriately. It makes them seem more heroic.	1	One half mark per correct answer. It is a useful starter to discuss what other words could be used. The poet chooses words that suggest a picture because they affect our senses.
8	Showers are fierce and short. The arrows from the Indians were falling around them in this fashion. Rain is also thin and falls vertically – this would give us an image of the density of the arrows and how they fall around the settlers. This would also tell us how dangerous the fight was. "fed them hot lead" refers to the bullets they were fighting with. The bullets would have been "hot" as they were being fired so quickly. They would have been "fed" as they ended up inside them.	2	Discuss the meaning of simile and metaphor. Talk about how pictures in the mind are created by the words used by writers.

Answers

Writing Test 2

The following criteria provide guidelines to help you gain an idea of your child's Writing level. A more precise numerical marking system is used by professional markers for marking National Tests.

Each level assumes that the criteria for the previous level have been met. Marks are out of 30.

Content (composition and effect)	Level
Is the writing in the correct form (for example, in an appropriate layout and in the correct person and tense)? Is fiction writing imaginative? Is non-fiction writing clear and does it have a logical structure?	Level 3
Is there an attempt to interest the reader? Is the style or viewpoint maintained throughout most of the writing? Are the criteria suggested on the planning sheet met?	Level 4
Is the tone of the writing maintained throughout? Is the language expressive and effective? Are the vocabulary and language appropriate for the purpose of the writing (for example, the use of technical or subject-based language, metaphors, similes or comparisons)? Are they suitable for the readers?	Level 5
Grammar and structure (sentence structure, punctuation and text organisation)	Level
Are the ideas presented in sequence, with full stops, capital letters, question marks and commas usually used correctly? Is a greater range of connective words and phrases used (for example, next, afterwards, so)?	Level 3
Are some of the sentences long, with correctly-used connective words and phrases (for example, meanwhile, however, which, that, who)? Are conditionals, such as if or because used? Do some sentences contain more than one verb or include commas, semi-colons, exclamation marks or speech marks? Are the tense and person consistent throughout? Does the structure of the text add to its effect?	Level 4
Are commas and speech marks used correctly throughout? Is a range of connective words and phrases used? Is a range of punctuation marks used correctly, including brackets or dashes and colons to separate parts of a sentence? Is the length of the sentences varied to express meaning? Are passive or active verbs used appropriately?	Level 5

Question number	Answer	Mark	Parent's notes and additional information
1	a. The swan <u>glided</u> across the lake. b. The mosquito <u>darted</u> in front of my eyes. c. The butterfly <u>fluttered</u> around the flower. d. The ducks <u>waddled</u> down the path. e. My cat <u>stalked</u> the mouse. f. The mouse <u>scurried</u> into the hole. g. The pony <u>trotted</u> into the farm. h. The snake <u>slithered</u> across the grass.	4	One half mark for each correct answer.
2	a. man/men b. goose/geese c. woman/women d. mouse/mice e. fish/fish	5	One mark for each correct answer.
3	knee – to kneel spark – to sparkle freedom – to free amusement – to amuse excitement – to excite	5	One mark for each correct answer.
4	For example: a. The racing car went out of control **when** it hit the barrier. b. I will get a new car **when** I am seventeen. c. I hope you can see **where** you are going. d. There was a huge snake in the grass **where** I was standing.	4	Answers can vary here – different options can occur – but the children should be using 'when' or 'where' correctly.
5	we are – we're; there is – there's; I will – I'll; cannot – can't; he is – he's; shall not – shan't; did not – didn't; they have – they've	4	One half mark for each correct answer.
6	friendly; nearly; luckily; happily; safely; thankfully; finally; simply	4	One half mark for each correct answer.
7	a. Cakes are made from flour, milk, butter and sugar. b. Freda ordered a burger, a large cola, a big bag of fries and a chocolate cake, before she was ill. c. Her sister is rude, lazy, silly and very good looking. d. As a gift I bought chocolates, ice-cream, flowers and a CD. e. In the box there were piles of books – old, dirty, dog-eared, smelly and unwanted – worth a fortune.	5	One mark for each correct sentence.
8	1. photo – light, e.g. photograph, photosynthesis 2. tele – from afar, e.g. telephone, television 3. bi – two, e.g. bicycle, bisect 4. circu – circular, round, e.g. circus, circumference	4	Answers can vary here - different options can occur - but the children should be using the prefix correctly.
9	1. He lifted the seat; the big spider crawled out. 2. Fred loves Chinese food; Sophie likes Indian food. 3. It was autumn; the nights were getting shorter. 4. I had lost the key; I would be in trouble. 5. Mum and Dad talked all through the holiday; they had not had time to chat before.	5	One mark for each correct sentence.
Total: divide by 2 so score is out of 20			

Assessment of children's attainment in National Curriculum tests depends upon the judgement of professionals. For the purposes of this book, a simplified system of marking is used. Guidelines to National Curriculum levels provided should be regarded as a rough guide only.

Use the conversion tables below to gain an idea of your child's National Curriculum Level.

English – reading		English – writing		English – grammar, punctuation and spelling		English – overall	
Level	Mark range	Level	Mark range	Level	Mark range	Level	Mark range
N	0–10	N	0–5	N	0–3	N	0–19
3	11–17	3	6–11	3	4–9	2	20–22
4	18–33	4	12–17	4	10–15	3	23–40
5	34–50	5	18–30	5	16–20	4	41–69
						5	70–100

Enter your child's results below:

English – reading	English – writing	English – grammar, punctuation and spelling	English – overall
Mark	Mark	Mark	Mark

Estimated National Curriculum Level: _____

Science at Key Stage 2

Most children at Key Stage 2 attain Levels 3 to 4 in Science, but some may attain Level 5. This performance at the different levels is summarised below.

Level 3	Level 4	Level 5
Children can describe differences and provide simple explanations. They can sort materials and living things and offer ideas about why materials are suitable for their purpose. When explaining how things work they link cause and effect, such as suggesting that the lack of light causes plants to become yellow. They also make generalisations about things they see, such as suggesting that it is difficult to see dim lights if they are near very bright lights.	Children can use more scientific terms such as the names of the organs of the body and those of flowering plants. They can use technical terms to describe processes such as evaporation and condensation. They can explain how differences are used to classify materials and living things systematically. They use their ideas about the way the physical world works when explaining how shadows are formed or the way that sound is heard through different materials.	Children can explain the factors behind why different organisms are found in different environments. They can describe the properties of metals and how they are distinct from other materials. They can identify why changes occur in materials and can suggest ways in which specific mixtures can be separated. They can use abstract ideas and models to explain physical phenomena such as the orbiting model of the earth to explain day and year length.

Setting the tests

This book contains two sets of practice papers. Give your child plenty of time to do each test — 45 minutes should be about right.

The tests can be a chance to confirm how well your child has done and how much he or she has learnt. Don't focus exclusively on what the child does not know.

Marking the tests

To mark the tests, enter the mark obtained in the circle next to each question. Add the marks together at the end of the test. Look at pages 115 and 125 for an indication of the National Curriculum Level at which your child is working.

Science Test 1

5

1   These animals all have backbones.

   a   Connect the animal to the group to which it belongs.

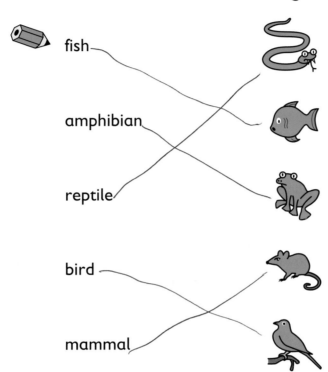

fish

amphibian

reptile

bird

mammal

   b   Connect the animal group to the description.

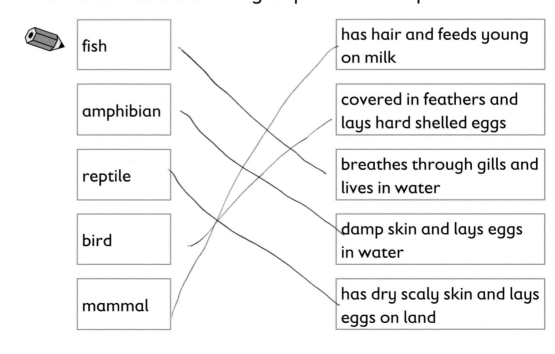

fish

amphibian

reptile

bird

mammal

has hair and feeds young on milk

covered in feathers and lays hard shelled eggs

breathes through gills and lives in water

damp skin and lays eggs in water

has dry scaly skin and lays eggs on land

5

TOTAL

10

2 Larry has a magnet on a string. There is a paper clip on a box. He uses the magnet to pull the box.

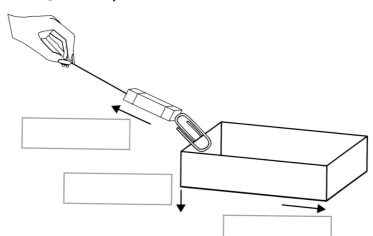

a Label the three forces on this box.

3

b Larry puts a 500 g mass into the box. The magnet no longer pulls the box. Explain why this has happened.

1

_____

_____

Food
chain

3 **a** Draw the arrows between the parts of this food chain.

| plankton | shrimps | fish | seals |

1

b Which is the producer in this food chain?

1

_____

c Name the two carnivores in this food chain.

1

_____

TOTAL

4 **a** Children wear out their trousers quickly. Terry wants to test denim and cotton cloth for toughness.

Tick the best way of doing this test.

Rub each one with a smooth piece of plastic. ☐

Rub each one with soap. ☐

Rub each one with a rough stone. ☑

1

b Write down one way to make the rub test fair for each cloth.

rub against the carpet

1

c Tom tested the hardness of three rocks.

	Can it be scratched with a coin?	Can it be scratched with a steel screw?
Sandstone	no	yes
Limestone	yes	yes
Granite	no	no

Write the names of the rock from softest to hardest.

Limestone   *Sandstone*   *Granite*

softest ———————————————→ hardest

1

d Pencil rubbers make holes in some paper when you rub hard. How would you test two types of paper to find the tougher paper?

Write your idea here.

Keep rubbing to penicl rubbers and see which makes a hole next

TOTAL

4

5 a Sam and his dad are making jam. They add sugar, water and strawberries. They boil the mixture.

What happens to the sugar?

I melts

1

b They measure the temperature of the boiling jam. Tick the correct instrument to use.

ruler ☐   spring balance ☐

stop clock ☐   thermometer ☑

1

c Tick the temperature you predict the jam would reach.

50°C ☐   105°C ☑   500°C ☐

1

6

metal   wood

a When making jam, the pan gets hot. Metal pan handles can get too hot.

Explain why metal pan handles get hot.

The pan is metal and it transfers the heat to the handle

1

b Wooden pan handles are usually cooler than metal handles.

Explain why wooden pan handles are usually cooler.

The pan is not wood and wood dosent transfer the heat like metal does

1

7 Sam and his dad pour the runny jam into the pots. They leave the pots for an hour. The jam cools down.

What other change to the jam takes place?

It hardens ever so slightly

1

TOTAL

6

Fish tank

8 Tim measured the temperature of the water in his fish tank. He used a sensor attached to a computer to record the changes.

This is Tim's temperature chart.

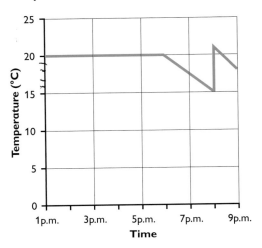

a How long was the sensor in the tank?

8 hrs

1

b What was the temperature of the water in the tank at first?

20°C

1

c What was the temperature of the water at 9 p.m.?

18°C

1

d Tim added some warm water to the tank. At what time did he do this?

8pm

1

e Fish tanks are made from glass or plastic. Give **two** reasons why these materials are used.

You can see the fish.

2

TOTAL

6

9 **a** Write a question that will sort these animals into two groups.

ladybird   bee   spider

What animal has six legs and what has eight.

b Gary has listed the stages in the life cycle of a frog. They are in the wrong order.

Number the sentences to show which order they should be in.
(The first has been done.)

The tadpoles change into frogs. | 4 |

The frogs grow larger. | 5 |

The eggs grow. | 2 |

The tadpoles hatch. | 3 |

The frogs mate and produce eggs. | 1 |

TOTAL

5

111

Temperature

10 Pam and Harry are dissolving white sugar in water.
They stir the mixture.
Harry thinks that sugar will dissolve faster in warm water
than in cold water.

3

a Write how you could test Harry's idea.

Remember to say what you will change.

I would use hot water and freezing
cold water

2

b Write **two** things you would keep the same to test
Harry's idea.

the sugar

spinning the water and sugar

3

c They had to measure temperature, time and amount
of sugar.
Draw a line from the instrument to what it measures.

spoon — time

thermometer — volume

stop clock — temperature

TOTAL

8

112

d They timed how quickly the sugar dissolved.
These are their results.

Temperature of water (°C)	Time taken for the sugar to dissolve (seconds)
20	100
30	80
40	60
50	40
60	

Use the grid below to draw a line graph using these results.

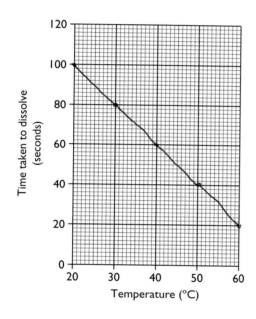

4

e They did not test water at 60 °C.
Predict how long it would take sugar to dissolve at 60 °C.

I predict it will take _____20_____ seconds for sugar to dissolve in water at 60 °C.

1

1

f Was Harry right?
Does sugar dissolve more quickly in warm water?

_____Yes_____

TOTAL

6

Answers

Science Test 1

Question number	Answer	Mark
1a	fish amphibian reptile bird mammal	5
1b	fish — has hair and feeds young on milk amphibian — covered in feathers and lays hard shelled eggs reptile — breathes through gills and lives in water bird — damp skin and lays eggs in water mammal — has dry scaly skin and lays eggs on land	5
2a	pull / gravity / friction	3 (1 mark for each correctly labelled)
2b	The friction (or forces stopping the box from moving) is now greater. It is more than the attraction of the paperclip to the magnet.	1
3a	plankton → shrimps → fish → seals	1
3b	plankton	1
3c	fish and seals	1
4a	Rub each one with a rough stone.	1
4b	A sentence or sentences conveying one or all of these ideas. I will rub in the same way for each cloth. I will use the same piece of stone for each cloth. I will make the same size hole in each cloth.	1
4c	limestone — sandstone — granite	1
4d	I would rub each one until it made a hole. *or* I would count the number of rubs needed to make a a hole. *or* I would rub as hard on each paper. *or* I would use the same rubber each time.	1 (1 mark for any one of these)
5a	It dissolves.	1
5b	thermometer	1
5c	105 °C (jam boils at a higher temperature than water)	1
6a	Metal is a good conductor of heat.	1
6b	Wood is not a good conductor of heat (accept wood insulates against heat / wood is a heat insulator).	1
7	The jam turns from a liquid to a solid as it cools.	1
8a	8 hours	1
8b	20 °C	1
8c	Approx 18 °C	1
8d	8 p.m.	1
8e	Plastic and glass are transparent or see-through and strong.	2
9a	Any question that distinguishes between insects and a spider, e.g. Does it have six legs? *or* Does it have eight legs? *or* Does it have one part to its body? *or* Does it have three parts to its body? *or* Does it have wings?	1

Question number	Answer	Mark
9b	The tadpoles change into frogs. 4 The frogs grow larger. 5 The eggs grow. 2 The tadpoles hatch. 3 The frogs mate and produce eggs. 1	4
10a	Pam and Harry should measure the time it takes sugar to dissolve. They should change the temperature of the water for each test.	3

10b	They should (accept any two):
	    stir each mixture at the same rate
	    use the same amount and sort of sugar for each test
	    use the same amount of water
	    use the same containers.
		2

10c	spoon time thermometer volume stop clock temperature	3
10d		4
10e	I predict it will take 20 seconds for sugar to dissolve in water at 60 °C.	1
10f	Yes it did. (You can see from the graph that sugar dissolved in 80 seconds at 30 °C and it only took 40 seconds at 50 °C.)	1

National Curriculum Levels

Science Test 1

Total marks 52

Mark	0–19	20–25	26–39	40–52
Level	Below 3	3	4	5

Swings

1 Pat makes a pendulum.

He times how long it takes to swing 10 times.

He changes the mass of the pendulum.

This table shows his results.

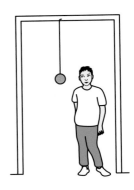

Mass of pendulum (grams)	Number of swings in 10 seconds
100	14
200	14
300	14

a What do you notice about the number of swings in 10 seconds?

_____

1

b Pat decides to change the length of the pendulum.

He shows his results on a line graph.

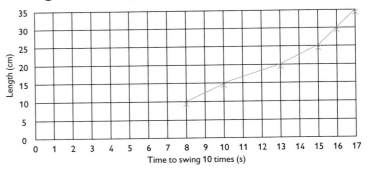

1

Tick the best explanation of these results.

☐ Long pendulums take a longer time to swing 10 times.

☐ Long pendulums take a shorter time to swing 10 times.

☐ The length of the pendulum does not affect the swing.

TOTAL

2

c   The children used three measuring instruments.
Write what each instrument measured.

Instrument	What did it measure?
Stopwatch	
Ruler	
Weighing scales	

3

d   The children play on swings in the park.
Pat and his dad sit on swings with chains the same length.
They let the swings go backwards and forwards.
Tick your prediction.

☐   They will swing at roughly the same rate.

☐   Pat's dad will swing more quickly

☐   Pat will swing much faster than his dad.

1

e   Pat sits on a swing with a shorter chain.
Predict what will happen.

☐   Pat will swing more slowly.

☐   Pat will swing at the same rate.

☐   Pat will swing more quickly.

1

TOTAL

5

2 Class 6 is making electrical circuits.

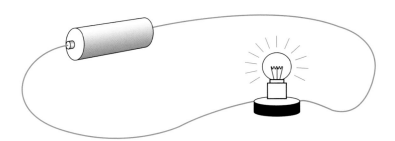

a Jane wants to make her bulb brighter.

Suggest one way she could increase the brightness of her bulb.

1

_____

b Harry wants to reduce the brightness of his bulb.

Suggest one way he could do this.

1

_____

c What electrical parts are shown in this circuit diagram?

Write the name of the part in the box.

1

d Explain why the motor in this circuit will not work.

1

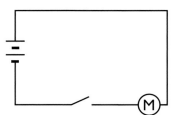

TOTAL

5

_____

3 What happens to these materials when they are warmed in an oven? Do they melt or stay unchanged?

a Put ONE tick in each row to show what happens.

Material	Melt	No change
ice cream		
steel		
margarine		
jelly		
brick		

5

b Joss freezes orange juice to make an ice lolly. When he takes the frozen lolly from the freezer, it melts. The change from liquid to solid has been reversed.

Some changes cannot be reversed.
They are irreversible.
Join each change to the correct label with a line.
Two have been done for you.

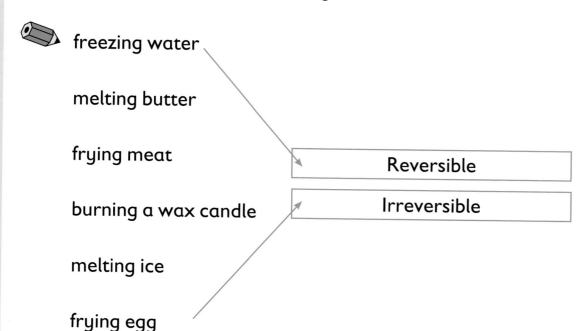

freezing water

melting butter

frying meat

burning a wax candle

melting ice

frying egg

Reversible

Irreversible

4

TOTAL

9

Fabric

4   Jim is testing four kinds of paper
to see which is most absorbent.
He times how long it takes for a
drop of water to soak in.
This is the bar chart of his results.

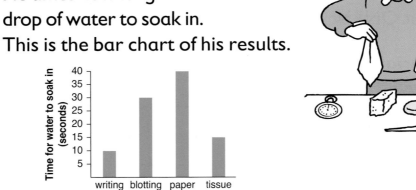

a   Which type of paper is most absorbent?

2

_____

_____

b   Which type of paper soaked up the water in 15
seconds?

2

_____

c   Suggest another test to see which type of paper is most
absorbent.

1

_____

_____

d   Say one way he could make his test fair for each type of
paper.

1

_____

_____

TOTAL

6

5   Kate and Ram are outside.
Kate taps the railing.
Ram is standing next to her but
can only just hear the tapping.

a   What is the sound travelling through to reach Ram?

_____

1

b   Ram puts his ear to the railing 5 metres away from
Kate.

This time he can hear the tapping much more clearly.
Name the **two** materials the sound passes through
this time.

_____

_____

2

c   Which of these two materials does sound travel
through best?

_____

1

d   Three children talk about
their ideas about sound
travelling. Put a tick in
the box beside the
one you agree with.

1

1

1

e   What evidence do you use to make your choice?

_____

TOTAL

6

Earth,
Sun and
Moon

6   a   This is a diagram of the Earth, Moon and Sun.
         Label this diagram with the correct words.

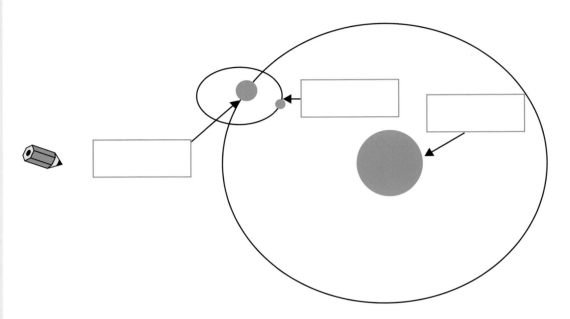

3

b   Join the words with the correct description.
    One line has been drawn.

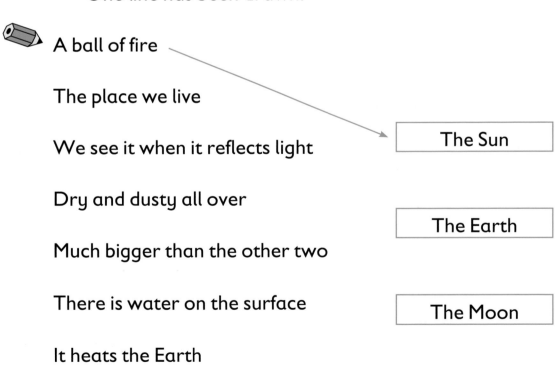

A ball of fire

The place we live

We see it when it reflects light   The Sun

Dry and dusty all over

Much bigger than the other two   The Earth

There is water on the surface

It heats the Earth   The Moon

3

TOTAL

6

7 **a** Some children are testing how high a tennis ball bounces.

They drop it from different heights onto a hard floor.

Height dropped from (cm)	Height bounced (cm)
50	25
100	50
150	75
200	

Predict what the last height will be. Write it in the table.

1

b Explain the pattern in these results.

_____

_____

1

c The children test the way the ball bounces on different surfaces.

They drop it from **100 cm** each time.

Draw a line to show how high you think the ball will bounce on different surfaces.

The first one has been done for you.

hard floor   20 cm

carpet   0 cm

cushion   50 cm

1

TOTAL

3

Answers

Science Test 2

Question number	Answer	Mark	Parent's notes and additional information
1 Swings			
a	It does not change / it is the same / it has no effect	1	
b	Long pendulums take a longer time to swing 10 times.	1	
c	Stopwatch – the time it takes to swing Ruler – the length of the string / pendulum Weighing scales – the mass of the pendulum / the weight of the pendulum	3	
d	They will swing at roughly the same rate.	1	
e	Pat will swing more quickly.	1	
2 Electricity			
a	She could: • add more batteries (cells) • use fresh batteries (cells) • change the bulb (for one with a lower rating)	1	A battery is, strictly speaking, a collection of cells. Bulbs designed to work with low voltage will glow much more brightly than bulbs designed to work with higher voltage.
b	He could: • reduce the number of batteries (cells) • use a lower voltage battery • add several other bulbs in series • put into the circuit a pencil lead or other material which resists the flow of electricity	1	The last two points amount to the same thing as the filaments of the bulbs resist the electricity. Children of this age are unlikely to talk about electrical resistance.
c		1 1	The bulb can also be called a lamp. The battery, in this instance, is actually one cell but allow either battery or cell.
d	The switch is open and the circuit is not complete.	1	Allow the circuit is not complete / the electricity cannot get round the whole circuit.
3 Changes			
a	ice cream – melt steel – no change margarine – melt jelly – melt brick – no change	5	
b	melting butter – reversible frying meat – irreversible burning a wax candle – irreversible melting ice – reversible	4	Try some of these experiments at home with your child, to demonstrate the ideas more clearly.
4 Paper			
a	paper towel	2	
b	tissue paper	2	
c	He could hold strips of different papers in water and see how much each soaks up. (This could also be weighed.) He could spill a measured amount of water on a table and see how easily it can be wiped up. Other immersion and weighing tests could be devised as well.	1	
d	He must do the same thing to each sample of paper. Each paper sample should be the same size. The same amount of water should be used for each test.	1	

Question number	Answer	Mark	Parent's notes and additional information
5 Sound			
a	The sound is travelling through the air to reach his ear. (Some children may correctly say it is also travelling through the railing but the sound is travelling through the air to the boy.)	1	
b	Metal and air.	2	
c	Metal. (This is because he can hear the sound much more clearly.)	1	
d	Larry: Sound travels through solids best.	1	
e	This will vary: Ram can hear better when he has his ear pressed to the railing. I can hear what is being said in a room better if I press my ear to the door! I have pressed my ear to the table and noticed I can hear noises through the wood.	1	Sound travels much better through solids than gases like air. When the ear is pressed against the railings, much of the sound is transmitted through the skull.
6 Earth, Moon and Sun			
a		1 for each correctly labelled	The sizes of these bodies are not to scale – the Sun is vastly bigger than the Earth.
b		Half a mark for each correct arrow – maximum available is 3 marks	
7 Bouncing balls			
a	100 cm bounce	1	
b	The greater the height you drop it from, the higher it bounces.	1	Some children might add: You double the height it bounces when you double the height you drop it from. *or* It bounces half the height it was dropped from.
c	hard floor — 20 cm carpet — 0 cm cushion — 50 cm	1	

National Curriculum Levels

Science Test 2

Total marks 42

Mark	less than 9	9–20	21–30	31–42
Level	Below 3	3	4	5

Notes